A Month of Prayer

A Month of Prayer

Five-Minute Meditations for a Deeper Experience of Prayer

W. DOUGLAS HOOD JR.

Includes Daily Prayers by LEO S. THORNE

Foreword by Greg Rapier
Afterword by Leo S. Thorne

RESOURCE *Publications* · Eugene, Oregon

A MONTH OF PRAYER
Five-Minute Meditations for a Deeper Experience of Prayer

Copyright © 2023 W. Douglas Hood, Jr. and Leo S. Thorne. All rights reserved. Except for brief quotations in critical publications or reviews, no part of this book may be reproduced in any manner without prior written permission from the publisher. Write: Permissions, Wipf and Stock Publishers, 199 W. 8th Ave., Suite 3, Eugene, OR 97401.

Resource Publications
An Imprint of Wipf and Stock Publishers
199 W. 8th Ave., Suite 3
Eugene, OR 97401

www.wipfandstock.com

PAPERBACK ISBN: 978-1-6667-8874-7
HARDCOVER ISBN: 978-1-6667-8875-4
EBOOK ISBN: 978-1-6667-8876-1

VERSION NUMBER 10/30/23

All Scripture quotations, unless noted otherwise, are taken from the Common English Bible, copyright 2011. Used by permission. All rights reserved.

Contents

Foreword by Greg Rapier | vii

Introduction | ix

Acknowledgments | xv

1	A Call to Prayer	1
2	Does Prayer Work?	4
3	Jesus' Prayer Basics	7
4	God Will Guide Us	10
5	Faith in Prayer	12
6	Audacious Prayer	14
7	When Faith Is Difficult	17
8	Victory on Our Knees	19
9	The Puzzle of Prayer	21
10	When Our Hearts Are Anxious	23
11	Is Belief in a Personal God Possible?	25
12	When God Seems Distant	27
13	Our Failure With Prayer	30
14	Prayer and Responsibility	33
15	The Great Wisdom of Prayer	36
16	How Can I Find God?	39

17	The Sound of God	42
18	The Fear of Insignificance	45
19	The Deepest Form of Prayer	48
20	Praying as Jesus Prayed	51
21	Hesitant Believers	54
22	When We Struggle	56
23	Difficulties with Prayer	59
24	When God Says No	62
25	The Most Basic Pattern of Prayer	65
26	Hindered Prayers	68
27	A High-Resolution Faith	71
28	A Life Trained by Christ	74
29	Where Battles Are Won	77
30	The Inner Circle	80
31	Ending Well	83

A Prayer for Easter | 87
A Prayer at Thanksgiving | 89
A Prayer at Christmas | 91
A Birthday Prayer | 93

Epilogue | 97
About the Authors | 99
Bibliography | 101

Foreword
Praying Up the Mountain

"The next day Jesus wanted to go into Galilee, and he found Philip. Jesus said to him, 'Follow me.'" John 1:43

There's a small Nepalese group, Sherpas, who are known to live and work along Mount Everest. They've spent considerable time around the mountain, and their lungs are accustomed to high altitudes. This region is their home. For the climbers who try to scale Everest, Sherpas are invaluable. They carry bags and set up camps. But their main role is to determine the most secure route and act as a guide and companion for the brave climbers who decide to scale the mountain.

Rev. Drs. W. Douglas Hood Jr. and Leo S. Thorne live and breathe Scripture. The Christian walk is central to their lives, the Bible part of their home. They know the terrain well. And in this book, *A Month of Prayer*, they map out a secure path for fellow sojourners along the way. One journey over thirty-one days.

There is a depth and richness to the prayers and meditations in this book that can only arise from two people who take seriously their walk with Christ and who have spent a lot of time on this route. These reflections are thoughtful and refreshingly honest about the obstacles that will arise. They confront head-on hazards like doubt, loneliness, helplessness, and fear. They pull from the news the most treacherous of terrain and reference the rocky soils of their own lives.

These struggles are part of the journey. And so rather than hand us a road map and abandon us, Doug and Leo, like good Sherpas, accompany us on the road. To this end, each day's reading consists of two parts. First, Doug meditates upon the nature of prayer and its impact on our lives. Second, Leo invites us into a time of guided prayer and reflection. In other words, Doug and Leo walk alongside us every step of the way. Throughout the journey, we can practically hear Doug and Leo coaching us from a few feet up the mountain, "Follow me, as I follow the way."

The apostle Paul in First Corinthians urges the early church to do the same, saying, "Follow my example, just like I follow Christ's." (1 Cor 11:1). This route is old as time, and, from the very beginning, even the most faithful of Christians have leaned upon the wisdom of guides. In this sense, Doug and Leo are simply an extension of this rich history, leaning upon centuries-old wisdom to guide travelers in our modern day and age.

Now, I should be clear: praying is not as difficult as scaling Everest. You do not need to be in any sort of physical or spiritual condition to begin this book. In fact, Doug and Leo approach the topic in a way that makes prayer look rather easy, as if prayer is the most natural thing in the world. Almost, you might say, as if we were created for it.

Yes, in these capable hands, prayer is simple. All that's required is a desire to walk with God and to know God more fully. Five minutes is all it takes, five minutes of sustained travel each day, and before you know it, you'll turn back around and look out over the distant vistas and realize just how high you've truly climbed. This is what happens when you have a good Sherpa, and—more importantly—this is what happens when you commit to a life of prayer.

Rev. Greg Rapier, Associate Pastor, First Presbyterian Church of Delray Beach

Introduction

Several years ago, my friend Michael Brown retired from the Marble Collegiate Church in New York City, where he was the senior minister. Retirement implores each of us to examine what we've gathered through our lives and careers, forcing us to choose which mementos we keep and which we must give away. For Michael, one of the most difficult decisions was what he would do with his professional library—a library built with considerable thought and care over forty years of ministry. Among his large, distinguished collection was approximately twenty volumes by Leslie D. Weatherhead, a Methodist pastor of another generation. These volumes had special value for Michael, and he could not simply dispose of them. Instead, he offered them to me.

This is not uncommon—passing to our children or dear friends those things that hold rich meaning for us but which we simply cannot possess any longer. My brother, Wayne, has our mother's wedding ring, and I have my father's wallet, which holds very old pictures of him as a child and of his parents—pictures that were to him of great nostalgic value. Nostalgia is a very natural, deep, and powerful emotion that resides in many of us. It reminds us from whence we come and provides a sense of identity and connection to things much larger than ourselves. But nostalgia can be dangerous! Nostalgia can entrap us in yesterday, in a yearning to return to the past. By idealizing the past, the present and future begin to grow dim.

INTRODUCTION

The apostle Paul identified these potential dangers in his First Epistle to the Christians in Corinth: "*God has prepared things for those who love him that no eye has seen, or ear has heard, or that haven't crossed the mind of any human being.*" (1 Cor 2:9) Though the Bible has a rich regard for remembering the past—particularly God's mighty acts—God desires that our faith be one that leans forward into the future. Paul seeks to assure the Christians in Corinth that the past, however rich our memories may be, is nothing compared to what is to come. God continues to be present in our lives, as God was present in our past. God continues to create, as God created in the past. Therefore, the practice of our faith is to lean forward, not backward, as some caught in nostalgia are apt to do.

Prayer is the primary practice of the Christian life. As Simon Chan observes, "One becomes a practicing Christian by practicing prayer."[1] Prayer is the one foundational practice upon which all other faith practices depend—it is an acknowledgment of God's presence and our desire to have a relationship with God. Prayer changes us, and it changes God. Prayer changes us by directing us from self-reliance to trust in God and God's purposes. While prayer does not change the nature of God, it does change how God directs God's power. A wonderful example of this is in the eighteenth chapter of Jeremiah, where God asserts that if the people of Israel change their behavior, then God will change what God had planned for them.

Today, many people are overwhelmed by feelings of fear and insecurity. They don't know what the future holds! They feel powerless to manage or change the unknown, and whatever they can't control, they've learned to fear. At its core, this is the essence of original sin: the desire to go through life on our own. Fiercely independent, we may love God, but we don't want to trust God with the navigation of our lives. That belongs to us, or so we wish it would be. The result is fear, fear of whatever unknown circumstances the future might bring. Paul asks that we let go of our

---

1. Chan, *Spiritual Theology*, 127.

Introduction

feeble attempts to grasp the future and trust it to God. For God does know the future!

Letting go of control over our lives begins with cultivating a robust life of prayer. But anyone who takes prayer seriously will encounter significant difficulties. The causes are numerous, and it is not my intention to address more than a few here in this introduction. In my ministry, I have noticed the number one difficulty people have with prayer is that they envision God as a big blue genie up in heaven who grants whatever wishes and desires we might have. But this reduces God to a cosmic grocery store, a resource to be used, exploited, and ultimately ignored when we're no longer in need. This is an infantile level of prayer! It isn't about building a relationship with God! I imagine such prayers make God feel used and God's relationship with us abused! And what happens if these prayers go unmet or unanswered? For many, they stop praying altogether.

Another difficulty is what one early church leader called "The Dark Night of the Soul."2 This is often a period following some progress in Christian growth. As with any progress, such as weight loss, we become addicted to positive movement forward. But if that movement forward seems to stall, we become discouraged—if measurable improvement is absent, we call it failure. Enthusiasm gives way to discouragement. Discouragement then gives way to surrender. Unfortunately, growth in our Christian lives has such periods when progress seems to elude us. Progress toward union with God seems to stall, and prayers seem to go nowhere. The soul experiences nightfall. As the sixteenth-century Spanish mystic Teresa of Avila counseled, it's during these nights that we need to persevere, to persist in prayer despite our contrary feelings. The darkness will eventually lift.3

Prayer begins as an intentional act before it becomes integrated into a way of life. This movement from act to habit may be best explained through an analogy. Early in my marriage, my wife asked me why I only addressed her by her name. I didn't use terms

---

2. Chan, *Spiritual Theology*, 135.
3. Chan, *Spiritual Theology*, 137.

of endearment so common in relationships, such as "sweetheart." I still don't know why I didn't. It wasn't an intentional decision. But it seemed important to her, so I became intentional. Early efforts to address my wife as "sweetheart" felt forced, even if they did express my feelings for her. But I continued anyway. Today I use that term of endearment as naturally as drawing my next breath. I can't recall when the intentional act became a natural expression. The same is true for a life of prayer. Prayer may be intentional and unnatural in the beginning, but it is important. Over time, a life of prayer will become part of the natural rhythm of your day.

As a natural rhythm of prayer is cultivated, a relationship develops—a relationship with God. God becomes so much more than the granter of desires. God becomes our confidant, someone who can be trusted to walk alongside us, particularly when that walk becomes difficult. Jesus demonstrated that level of trust in his Heavenly Father even when he sweat drops of blood from fear in the garden of Gethsemane. The apostle Paul now urges us to have that same relationship with Jesus.

The Newlywed Game was a popular television show in the late sixties and early seventies that pitted newly married couples against each other by asking them questions about how well one knew the other. There would be two rounds; the wives were taken off stage first, while the husbands were asked three questions. The wives were then brought back into the studio and asked for their answers to the same three questions. Once the wife gave her answer, the husband revealed the answer he gave—written on a blue card—in her absence. Five points would be awarded to the couple that shared the same answer. The roles were reversed in round two, and the wives were asked to answer questions about their husbands and so on. The couple with the highest score at the show's end won.

Imagine a similar game that tests how well we know God and how well we understand God's purpose for our lives. I suspect many of us would be embarrassed. In Luke's Gospel, the disciples came upon Jesus when he was praying. Tremendously moved by what they saw, the disciples asked him to teach them to pray. Pay

INTRODUCTION

close attention: there is no hint in this passage that the disciples witness God answering Jesus' prayers. Real or hypothetical results weren't what caught their imagination. There was something else, something that went much deeper.

If we dispense with the notion that prayer is only about answers, that prayer is simply presenting pleas when we are in need, in danger, or in a crisis, our eyes are cleared to see what the disciples saw when they came upon Jesus at prayer. In Jesus' prayer, the disciples saw a concentration and absorption into a relationship with God that they had no experience with. Jesus' prayers demonstrated a deliberate and sustained cultivation of a relationship with God that would put Jesus in the winner's seat of *The Newlywed Game*. What is clear in Luke's Gospel is that the disciples wanted the same.

Perhaps the greatest difficulty with prayer today is that many are simply out of touch with God. Prayer is reduced to a mindless, meaningless habit rather than a sincere effort to cultivate a personal relationship with our creator. And that is our deepest need—to renew our acquaintance with God. J. Wallace Hamilton writes, "People say they don't pray because God is not real to them, but the truth is the other way around: God is not real to them because they do not pray."4 The goal of the Christian life is not self-improvement or moral perfection, nor is it to produce more saints. The goal of the Christian life is union with God.

Many struggle to experience such a union. They simply don't stay with prayer long enough for such a relationship to develop. Or, possibly, their understanding of the practice of prayer is limited. Consequently, they participate in the worship and ministry of the church but harbor quiet jealously of others who seem to experience a wondrous reservoir of joy absent in their own life. The meditations collected within this slim volume were written over nine years. They represent my own probing of the Scriptures to uncover the vast riches of the nature, practice, and power of prayer. Captured in the meditations are insights that made my own understanding of prayer more expansive while simultaneously

---

4. Hamilton, *What about Tomorrow*, 121.

INTRODUCTION

reflecting on the sufferings, struggles, and events of the weeks in which they were written. They have been collected here as originally presented.

In my personal life, I have found that distractions interfere with careful listening to God. Therefore, as you delve into this book, identify a time of day when you might spend a minimum of ten minutes alone with this resource and God. Five minutes will be for reading a single meditation along with its prayer of the day, and five minutes will be for stillness, reflecting upon what God may be saying to you through the words you've read. Try praying, "God, what would you have me hear?" and "What would you have me do?" The reader will benefit from reading this book as it is designed: one meditation a day for thirty-one days. Plowing through the book in one or two sittings will only diminish the value of any one of them. *A Month of Prayer* is not a book to be read as it is a collection of daily meditations that cultivate, slowly and over time, a deeper experience of prayer.

With this collection of meditations and prayers, Leo Thorne and I hope to provide a pathway to a deeper experience of prayer—an experience that flows organically from a deeper grasp of what Scripture teaches on the form, content, and practice of prayer. Herman Melville, the author of the novel *Moby Dick*, observed that "to produce a mighty book, you must choose a mighty theme."[5] The mighty theme of Jesus' life was prayer. Prayer requires time to cultivate; prayer demands extraordinary perseverance. But once Jesus' approach to prayer is mastered, don't be surprised if another approaches you and asks, "Teach me to pray like that."

---

5. Melville, *Moby Dick*, 487.

Acknowledgments

This book was prepared within a community—the staff of First Presbyterian Church of Delray Beach. For eleven years now, I have been given the good fortune of working alongside colleagues—each remarkably talented people—who all share a passion for elevating the church's witness of Jesus Christ and producing the greatest impact for Christ in the local community. The joy and enthusiasm of the staff is palpable. Those who worship on Sunday mornings notice and speak of it. Positive energy flows continuously, and stories are shared among one another of lives that are impacted by the work we do together each day. This is the environment in which these pages were prepared. This book is dedicated to each of them with gratitude.

Caroline Calder, Donald Cannarozzi, Christine Davis, Jessica Davis, Abigail Eccles, Nancy Fine, Birgit Djupedal Fioravante, Grace Cameron Hood, Liz Landis, Jenny Mullin, Greg Rapier, Nathan Singjaidee, Aaron Strippel, and Ashlyn Strippel.

The preaching ministry of the church has experienced strength upon strength from the two pastors, now retired, who have made this church their spiritual home, Drs. Leo and Yvonne Thorne. Each brings a unique voice to the pulpit, has exercised leadership within the church in other capacities, and shares in the wondrous impact of lives changed by this community of faith. This church and everyone who worships here is the richer for the two of them. I am particularly honored to share the preparation of this book with Dr. Leo Thorne.

Acknowledgments

I owe much to Nancy Fine, the business administrator of the church and a close friend. She has carefully read each line of this book, provided editorial suggestions for clarity, and prepared the manuscript for publication. Simply, without Nancy's careful attention to detail and care in preparing the manuscript to the exacting standards of the publisher, there would be no book.

I especially want to acknowledge my wife, Grace, and our two children, Nathanael and Rachael, who continue to bless me each day. Grace continues to demonstrate what a close walk with Jesus looks like, and my faith is strengthened daily by her own. Nathanael and Rachael, though you both have pursued careers far from home, you are never far from my heart.

To you, the reader of this book, I am grateful that you are inclined to pursue a deeper experience of prayer. Perhaps, by God's grace, this modest collection of meditations may be helpful as you create room in your life for God. As Terence E. Fretheim so eloquently puts it, "prayer creates more relational space for God, gives God more room in which to work, makes God more welcome."[1]

---

1. Fretheim, "To What Kind of God," 15.

1

A Call to Prayer

"Early in the morning, well before sunrise, Jesus rose and went to a deserted place where he could be alone in prayer." Mark 1:35

My grandmother kept a large, white, faux leather cover Bible prominently in her home—usually on a coffee table, though she would occasionally move it about her home as though it was a traveling exhibit. Embossed into the cover was a full-color picture of Jesus kneeling by a great rock in the wilderness. Each time my eyes fell upon that Bible, I felt as though it was a call to prayer. The face of Jesus was not anxious, not desperate as my own on those occasions I did pray. His face portrayed confidence, a radiance one has in the company of loved ones who care deeply about us. Absent was worry, doubt, or any trace of anxiety that threatened to consume. Yes, a call to prayer was evident in this picture of Jesus. However, that call made me uncomfortable—uncomfortable because I would experience a lack of spiritual power. With the disciples, I heard my own heart say, "Lord, teach us to pray like that."

In this Scripture, Jesus had just finished a hard, demanding day. Another day of similar demands stretched before him. How could Jesus be ready for it? Mark's Gospel gives us the answer and, with it, important insight into Jesus' power, "Early in the morning, well before sunrise, Jesus rose and went to a deserted place where he could be alone in prayer." Jesus was intentional with prayer. Jesus wove into the fabric of each day a time to be alone with God. Jesus regarded this time as a vital part of the human experience. Prayer was an opportunity to link his life with the purposes of God and cultivate a friendship with God. This friendship produced the confidence that Jesus would not face any of life's demands alone. That would be the source of Jesus' spiritual power.

My lack of spiritual power as a child was from an inadequate view of prayer. I had reduced prayer to those occasions when I would ask God for a favor or for help with a difficulty. Consequently, days without prayer would pass—I simply did not have any request to make of God. Yet, as I matured, I continued to pay attention to that picture on my grandmother's Bible, that picture of Jesus at prayer. It grew upon my consciousness that prayer is the same as time spent with a friend or loved one. I may not have anything to ask of my friend, but I did enjoy their company. I felt valued by them, loved by them, and strengthened because of their friendship. The same happens with prayer—a strong hand on the shoulder and the confidence to face each day swelling within. Power comes as we find ourselves surrounded by God's love, guidance, and strength.

With this refreshing surge of power that flows from regular time in prayer, it is very strange then that we should be content with so little prayer. The weakest, most fearful individual can experience greater strength through the regular rhythm of prayer each day. As this passage of Scripture demonstrates, prayer each day for Jesus was as ordinary as enjoying a meal. Jesus prayed often. Jesus prayed for himself and for others. Jesus prayed when he faced a crisis, and Jesus prayed simply to be alone with God. Jesus urged his disciples to pray, and Jesus taught prayer by example. What the disciples discovered is that regular prayer did not only sustain Jesus' ministry; it gave direction. Immediately after Jesus rose from prayer this particular morning, Jesus knew what he must do that day. He was not to return to the previous day's work. Jesus was to head in the other direction. God had new work for him there.

Gracious God, may your beautiful, life-giving radiance be seen in me today, in the way I speak and listen; in the way I share moments with family, friends, and colleagues; in the way I spend quiet time with you during the day. Shine, Jesus, shine through me today and give my life the holy assurance of being always with you at work or play. May the spiritual blessings of your love surround me today. I make this prayer in your strong and sustaining name, Jesus. Amen.

2

Does Prayer Work?

"While Peter was held in prison, the church offered earnest prayer to God for him. The night before Herod was going to bring Peter's case forward, Peter was asleep between two soldiers and bound with two chains, with soldiers guarding the prison entrance." Acts 12:5–6

Albert Einstein once commented to Phil Blackwood, a friend of mine, that to continue to do something in the same way and to expect different results is the definition of insanity. I suspect the difficulty so many people have with prayer is that it doesn't seem to work—at least not to their expectations. To continue to practice prayer with apparently little effect leads to discouragement and disillusionment. Eventually, they draw the same conclusion as Einstein—continuing to do something the same way and expecting different results is the definition of insanity. I once heard a story of an English author who wrote of his prayers to God at an early age. He prayed hard for something to happen. It didn't. Concluding that prayer doesn't work, he offered one final prayer, "All right, Mr. God. I won't bother you again."

That English author's story is often our story. We pray for something to happen. It doesn't. We stop trying. Perhaps we are not as blunt with God as the English author, but that is what happens. Some of us may persist in prayer longer than others, always praying in the same manner, "God, please heal my friend," or "God, help me with my finances," or "God, give back to the Miami Dolphins a winning season," and nothing happens. The friend doesn't get better, finances remain a difficulty, and the Miami Dolphins repeat another losing season. The result is that we quietly stop praying. Why bother God any further? The problem is we have misunderstood Einstein. He doesn't suggest we stop trying. Einstein is telling us to try another approach.

An episode of *Law & Order* presents a family torn apart by a husband and father who abandoned his family. He simply doesn't want the responsibility a family will demand. The son grows up to be a professional baseball player who is quite good with a handsome salary. The father reenters the son's life with excuses for why he abandoned the family. They are, naturally, unconvincing. Yet, the son is grateful to have a father in his life. Grateful, that is, until the son learns that the father has a gambling problem and needs rather large sums of money to cover gambling debts. In a heart-wrenching series of events, we learn that the father is too busy to accept an invitation to the son's home for dinner and to meet his daughter-in-law and grandchild, too busy to attend one of his son's ball games, and too busy to remember his son's birthday. Yet, the father is never too busy to "drop in" on his son for a handout to cover gambling debts.[1]

Often, that is our approach to God. Our lives are simply too busy to spend time with God in any meaningful manner. Nevertheless, we find the time to "drop in" on God when we have a need. The disciple Peter shows us another approach. Peter has been arrested and placed in prison. Herod had James put to death, and Peter knows that this was Herod's intention again. Placed in chains and guarded by sixteen soldiers, Peter goes to sleep. How can anyone sleep when there is a death sentence on his or her head? Peter

---

1. Sherin, *Law & Order*.

can. That is because he has lived so deeply into a relationship with Jesus that nothing frightens him anymore. Peter is changed by an approach to prayer that is more about growing intimate with God than receiving anything. Prayer's ultimate goal is to lead us into the presence of God, where we are changed. It is then we find peace, even when chained in a prison cell.

Dear God, prayer helps me stay close to you and to continue believing that I have worth. You understand every detail of my life, even in those moments when life is not calm and bright; when I question your love and my value in this world; when life in my family needs repair; and when I question that you are a good God in a world of so much trauma-producing suffering. Help me to trust in your unfailing strength and your wisdom, compassionate God, and to name what is the real barrier between you and me. In the powerful and sustaining name of Jesus, I make this prayer. Amen.

3

Jesus' Prayer Basics

"But when you pray, go to your room, shut the door, and pray to your Father who is present in that secret place. Your Father who sees what you do in secret will reward you. When you pray, don't pour out a flood of empty words, as the Gentiles do. They think that saying many words they'll be heard. Don't be like them, because your Father knows what you need before you ask." Matthew 6:6–8

What does Jesus say about prayer? It is important to return to Jesus' teaching, as there is much foolish talk about prayer. Some of that talk is in its favor but develops in directions unknown to Jesus, such as finding the right structure or cadence that elevates the effectiveness of prayer. Other talk appeals to reason that suggests that prayer only shapes a positive mental attitude and no more. Neither conversation is helpful for a person of faith—a person who believes the Jesus of the Bible continues to be available to God's people today as the risen Christ. In this teaching on prayer in Matthew's Gospel, Jesus assumes that God's people will pray. On that assumption, Jesus makes two common sense observations—two basics of effective prayer.

Jesus first asks that any prayer be a sincere prayer. Honest, genuine prayer is a conversation with God, no one else. Prayer that is offered in a manner that hopes for or anticipates an audience is not authentic. Rather than a conversation with God, such prayer is for show. God's response to prayer is of little importance—if at all. What is sought is the adulation and praise of another. The dominant desire is to advance a positive impression upon those who are near when the prayer is spoken. According to Jesus, the reward that is offered by the audience will be the only response to such prayers. God is not the primary audience of such prayers, so a response from God should not be expected.

Second, we must not indulge in repetitions—repeating a prayer over and over as though the flood of words will make a deeper impression on God. Jesus tells us that such repetitions become "empty" words. God will not be forced by such a pattern of prayer. Saying a prayer twenty, fifty, or a hundred times cannot unlock God's gracious movement toward us. God desires a relationship, not one that is manipulated or cajoled by the repetition of pious expressions. Once again, Jesus is appealing to our common sense, appealing to us to approach God as we would a close friend. It would be ridiculous to approach anyone we are close to with a request that is made over and over again. That simply would not be very pleasing.

Prayer is communion with God. The aim of prayer is a deeper relationship with God—not drawing the attention of others or supposing the God who placed the stars in the sky and every living thing upon the earth can be harnessed by pious phrases. Jesus wants us to know that if we desire to draw near to God, that desire must come from a sincere heart. Standing in a public place while praying, seeking the notice of others, and searching for some magical formula to draw God's attention isn't sincere. Nor would we use either approach to draw near someone we cared about. A heart that is affectionate, attentive, and genuine is one that captures the same from another. This is the prayer that captures the heart of God.

Dear God, I open my heart childlike to you today. I do not have many words to speak. I just want to be still with heart-to-heart communication. You are my reward. I worship you, merciful God. I make this prayer in the name of Jesus, my loving Savior. Amen.

4

God Will Guide Us

"Trust in the Lord with all your heart; don't rely on your own intelligence. Know him in all your paths, and he will keep your ways straight." Proverbs 3:5–6

The fall semester of my senior year in college would be in England. Arriving at Gatwick Airport in London, I disembarked the flight, entered the airport, and immediately experienced considerable confusion. Standing in a common area, bewildered by the signage, I felt a hand on my shoulder: "This is the direction you want to go," spoke a friendly voice. The confusion cleared, my path was made clear, and I was on my way. I am reasonably intelligent, but that moment was when I desperately needed guidance.

Anyone honest about their own life journey admits moments where guidance is welcomed. It is no mistake that high schools, colleges, and universities have "guidance counselors" available to their students. Determining a direction in life is not something to be decided casually. Nor is it a simple matter of discerning God's desire and direction for us as individuals. There are moments when we are as bewildered as I was when I stood in Gatwick Airport many years ago.

These words from Proverbs provide help. Rather than be intimidated by the vastness of choices and decisions to be made, Proverbs invites us into a relationship with our creator. This relationship moves from the mind to the heart. There is a critical difference. The mind alone gathers information, orders data, and considers several reasonable alternatives. The entire exercise can be accomplished without ever disturbing the heart from its sleep. On the other hand, try building a relationship with a spouse or friend solely on the arrangement of data. It doesn't work. The heart senses, feels, and longs to know and be known. There is the knowledge that is simply unavailable using the mind alone.

How shall we trust and know God with all our heart? We begin by learning of God as God is revealed in the Bible. We continue by doing God's will as best as we understand it from our reading. There is no substitution or shortcut. Divine guidance only comes to those who seek it daily in the Scriptures. We become sensitive to the nudges and promptings of God until, one day, we sense a hand on our shoulder and a voice that speaks, "This is the direction you want to go."

God of all-knowing, let me walk together with you in sweet relationship today, not in front of you lest I lose my way; not behind you, because at times, I want to see more than I need to see. Help me to walk hand-in-hand, side-by-side, with you in a delightful, trusting friendship. And, dear God, maybe today, I can encourage someone to find you as their loving friend. Thank you for being my unfailing Guide. I make this prayer in the strong name of Jesus the Christ. Amen.

5

Faith in Prayer

"Jesus was telling them a parable about their need to pray continuously and not to be discouraged." Luke 18:1

I believe in prayer. I believe that prayer is the most important fact in the life of anyone who is determined to follow Jesus. The trouble with prayer is not belief in the practice—it is what is expected from it. For many, prayer is practiced as some sort of holy magic. Pray correctly and with enough faith, and the desired result arrives every time. Unanswered prayer is simply the result of praying incorrectly or with insufficient faith. This belief is troubling, if not downright harmful, to a person of faith. In this sentence from Luke's Gospel, Jesus teaches that we are to "pray continuously." Rather than suggesting yet another formula for prayer—pray continuously—I believe our Lord is inviting us to discover at least two ways that prayer is effective.

On one level, prayer opens the one who is praying to a relationship with God. Meaningful relationships are not built by one or two sentences that are shaped into a request, not with God or anyone else. "Continuous prayer" is the cultivation of a regular conversation with God. This is the kind of conversation between two people caring for one another. Whether we are angry or thankful, whether we are sharing from a broken heart or celebrating, we share continuously with those whom we love. Such conversations draw us closer to one another. It is that closeness with us that God desires.

A second level involves the one for whom we pray. By our prayers, that person is not alone. Continuous prayer keeps them in the fellowship of our thoughts and our hearts. A community of faith is created, which liberates them from walking a difficult path unaccompanied by someone who cares. Encouragement and strength bubble forth when we know that there is someone who is pulling for us. Creating community among people of faith is one result of continuous prayer.

Faith in prayer does not exclude expectations of the miraculous. God is still in the miracle business. But we are guilty of a grievous error when we reduce prayer to "getting what we want." That makes God a dispenser of religious goods and services while we continue to build the life we want apart from God's claim upon us. Christian prayer is always undergirded by a conviction that God is reconciling us to God's self for the purpose of being used by God for God's ongoing work in the world. "Continuous prayer" is an affirmation that our life is not ours to do as we wish. We belong to God, and it is for God that we live.

Heavenly Friend, help me to learn the difference between saying prayers and praying. I am growing to understand that praying invites a two-way conversation in your presence, Lord, when heart meets heart. Praying encourages me to wait on you to hear your still, small voice deep in my soul. Praying draws me to listen with my spirit for your Holy Spirit and know that you are in this space with me. Continue to teach me, Lord, that prayer is about building an ongoing life that is never apart from you and your loving participation in my life. Heavenly Father, help me to experience you, my God, beyond the words I say. I pray in the strong name of Christ. Amen.

6

Audacious Prayer

"Finally, let's draw near to the throne of favor with confidence so that we can receive mercy and find grace when we need help." Hebrews 4:16

A simple story that is repeated often each day throughout the world is that of a father seated in his home, reading a book, a magazine, or a newspaper. A young son enters the room and climbs-up into his father's lap. The father, with a warm heart, asks, "Well, what can I do for you?"

"Nothing," replies the son. "I just want to be with you."

Prayer may be many things. Yet, in the final analysis, prayer—true prayer—is not the utterance of words nor the advance of desires but the desire to be with God. Prayer is not a formal, religious exercise or a vocal performance before others. It is deeper than that. Prayer is spiritual communion with the creator of heaven and earth. From beginning to end, prayer's aim is to experience the presence, affirmation, and love of one greater and stronger than us. To know we are safe in their arms.

The book of Hebrews teaches us that access to God is only possible through Jesus. Prayer will not prevail without the Son of God who made possible the removal of the veil that separated us from the holy throne of God. John Calvin, an early Protestant leader of the Christian faith, asserts that prayer is fundamentally acknowledging the continuing intercession of Jesus Christ.[2] Jesus must go with us as we draw near the "throne of favor," the seat of Almighty God. Without Jesus, we remain shut out from the living God. As Jesus taught us in the Lord's Prayer, prayer must always begin with the acknowledgment that we come to a holy, sacred place, to "uphold the holiness of your name" (Matt 6:9). We must not forget this. Therefore, when we pray, we come not only before a Heavenly Father but we also come into a royal place of power.

If we come to a throne, our posture must be that of deep reverence. Continuing today is the demonstration of respect and reverence as world leaders come before a king or queen—reverence demonstrated by a simple bow. It may be a bow of the head or a bow from the waist. Yet, what is expected is that any approach before royalty is accompanied by homage and honor. In the instance of prayer, the royal one we approach is the highest of all royalty, the King of kings. (1 Tim 6:15). Thomas Long, a wise interpreter of Scripture, writes that sometimes contemporary Christians, schooled on a tame and domesticated picture of God, forget the sheer audaciousness of human beings daring to approach the holy, and thus we engage in prayer with all the casual nonchalance of ordering at a fast-food restaurant.[3]

Though we come before "the throne of favor" with humility and reverence, we do come before a throne. Small change found in the sofa and leftover crumbs are not dispensed in a place of royalty. More, we are present before God at God's invitation; we are called God's children. That knowledge removes any hesitancy to ask God for anything. That knowledge also removes any expectation that all we can hope for are small favors—small coins or breadcrumbs. God's invitation suggests that we are to appear with enlarged expectations! Yet, beware of imagining that God's thoughts are our thoughts or that God's ways are our ways. Ask for great things

[2] Barth, *Prayer*, xiii.
[3] Long, *Hebrews*, 64.

because you stand before a great God. But always pray as Jesus prayed, "let it be what you want" (Matt 26:42).

    God Almighty, I give you thanks for the privilege and delight of being invited into your holy presence. You are my God, and today I want to enjoy being in your spiritual presence. I gently push to the side all my prayer requests. I patiently wait here with you, righteous God, in holy reverence; in reflective respect; in the joy of your Holy Spirit who lives and works in me; and in the spirit of heartfelt praise for your amazing grace to me. Surprise me with your still, small voice today, and then give me the generosity and courage to go out and surprise someone today with a simple act of love. In the powerful name of Jesus, I pray. Amen.

7

When Faith Is Difficult

"We can't find goodness anywhere." Psalm 4:6

If there remains anyone who argues that the Bible isn't relevant for today, they have demonstrated that they haven't paid attention to the Bible—not close attention, anyway. Is there anything more timeless than the agonizing cry "we can't find goodness anywhere"? Each morning our minds are disturbed by the growing threat of the militant Islamic group, ISIS, the conflict between Israel and Palestine, and the racial unrest in Ferguson, Missouri. Beneath these attention-getting headlines is the less-mentioned but continuing concern of the growing wealth gap in our country and the millions in our nation who struggle daily to simply have enough. There are no snappy answers to the painful question of human struggle.

It is well that the Bible does not offer a quick and prefabricated answer to this despairing cry. And it is best for us to refrain from such a temptation. First, we are not free to indulge in cynical or dismissive attitudes such as "well, that's life," or "bad things just happen." As followers of Jesus, we are baptized into the common confession that our lives are in the hands of God and that this God is a God of love. Second, we don't occupy some place between God and humanity's struggle. Not one of us has some special insight into the mysterious work of God in the midst of our common difficulty. Each of us must sweat it out with everyone else.

What remains is a prayer: "Lord, show us once more the light of your face." This is the prayer of the Psalmist, and nothing new can be added. The prayer is the same today as it was yesterday, fresh and urgent. It is as new as the earthquake that shook the San Francisco Bay Area a few days ago and the agony that kept someone awake last night. It is new when we utter it personally today. No devotional, not one inspirational book can answer the plea, the emotional depth of that prayer.

On our knees, we pray. If we listen in the silence between our words, the Holy Spirit reminds us that God was never absent in the horrors of human life in the Bible—nor will God be absent today. On the Via Dolorosa—the way of the cross—in Jerusalem, God was very present in the heart of human misery, giving, giving, and giving himself so that after this, there would be no fear, no despair, and no doubt of God's love. The cry "we can't find goodness anywhere" still sounds in the streets of our communities. We live with it, and we hear it echo in our souls. But the spirit helps us recall the suffering of Christ—a suffering accepted out of Christ's love for us. It is a love that will work for the good of all those who love him.

Ever present, all-wise God, help me to get a handle today on your unconditional and amazing love for me. Your word teaches me that the life I live with you is by faith, not by sight. Help me to peer through those welcoming nooks and crannies of your love and see your goodness and broken heart in life's painful and difficult moments. Jesus, you came to earth to help me look again at the human condition through your harmless and forgiving eyes of love. May your love encourage every breath I breathe today. In the name of your risen Christ, I pray. Amen.

8

Victory on Our Knees

"I live on high, in holiness, and also with the crushed and the lowly, reviving the spirit of the lowly, reviving the heart of those who have been crushed." Isaiah 57:15

Recently Grace and I spent a weekend in the Florida Keys with two dear friends. In addition to sharing meals together, shopping, stimulating conversation about our families, and an evening of bicycling, the four of us summoned the courage to try something we had never done before—paddleboarding. The sport's popularity seems to be growing exponentially in South Florida, particularly the Keys. It looked fun and appeared to be a sport that would be easy for beginners. It was not. Paddleboarding challenges both core strength and balance, and beginners spend more time falling from the board than standing. My wife, Grace, was perhaps an exception; other people asked me how long she had been paddle boarding.

After several attempts at standing—and failing—Grace said to me to begin on my knees: "You have more control on your knees." Hearing my wife's words, my friend commented, "I hear a sermon in there somewhere!" Naturally, I was frustrated that I was unable to master paddleboarding immediately. But then, where would have been the satisfaction in that? Satisfaction with life is often preceded by considerable effort and discipline. So it is with our Christian faith. We must experience failure on our own before we can value God's presence and strength that enables us to stand. The pinnacle of joy and satisfaction in our faith is our communion with the risen Christ. That communion begins on our knees in prayer—demonstrating that we can't do life apart from God.

To be a Christian is to follow Jesus. And his own life was no leap from the cradle in Bethlehem to the victory of Easter morning. Victory implies something was defeated. Between birth and resurrection, Jesus lived deeply. It was a life that knew suffering, betrayal, and abandonment. We experience with Jesus the victory and joy of the resurrection because we know all too well his hell of loneliness and pain. It was a hell that Jesus defeated because he spent so much of his life on his knees. Grace is absolutely right: "You have more control on your knees."

The central question that confronts many today is where is God in the darkness of the present world—the darkness that seems to defeat a hope for tomorrow? Isaiah declares that our God lives with the crushed and the lowly. God is not only present in our darkness; God is at work, "reviving the spirit of the lowly, reviving the heart of those who have been crushed." God did so for Jesus. God will do so for us. What is needed is that we wait for God's victory on our knees.

Blessed God, I am trying to remember the last time I spent quality time on my knees with you. And did my knees hurt then? No pain, no gain; no bending, no standing up; no falling, no rising; no surrender, no victory; no cross, no crown; no weeping at night, no joy in the morning; no eyes closed, no insight. May my prayer experience today remind me of the power and victory Jesus received when in submission he prayed, not for his will to be done, but yours. In Jesus' name. Amen.

9

The Puzzle of Prayer

"We always thank God for all of you when we mention you constantly in our prayers." 1 Thessalonians 1:2

It is not unusual for someone to ask me, "Please pray for me." Often my response is an invitation to immediate prayer. My desire is to take the request for prayer seriously. By praying with the person immediately, I wish to say that I care deeply about them and that I appreciate their confidence in the power of prayer. Recently, however, I have begun to question, "Just what do they expect from this prayer? Do they really believe my prayer to do any good?"

Naturally, the Bible has much to say about prayer. What is often unrealized is just how frequently the mention of prayer in the Bible is one of complaint. The palmists, the prophets, Job, and the apostle Paul often questioned the value of prayer, sometimes rather bluntly! Listen to a portion of Ps 88: "But I cry out to you, Lord! My prayer meets you first thing in the morning! Why do you reject my very being, Lord? Why do you hide your face from me?" (Ps 88:13–14). It is clear that today's church is not the first to question the usefulness of prayer.

It is important—and helpful—to note, however, that in each complaint that is uttered, there is present a fervent belief that something can be expected from prayer. Prayer is never given up on in the Bible, never dismissed as not of any use. What makes each of those who wrestle with prayer people of amazing stature is their absolute confidence in the power of prayer—the power to disrupt at any moment the ordinary with the extraordinary. Without reserve or embarrassment, each character in the Bible shared the same compulsion to pray.

I will freely share that I have no idea how prayer works. The question itself may be foolish simply because it strives to understand God. And someone once wisely declared that if we can ever grasp God, then we must go looking for another God. Any God we can understand with our finite minds is simply too small to save us. What I am confident of is that God was very active in the drama recorded in the Bible and continues to be just as involved in the unfolding drama of life today. And God invites us, repeatedly, to seek the inflow of God's grace through regular prayer. Refusal to pray—even when prayer was questioned—simply was not an option for the people of faith in the Bible.

God of mystery and power, may my heart truly expect an answer for my prayer today, your answer. I pray with thanksgiving, and I will go out today and have some fun, even as I live with the questions. Amen.

10

When Our Hearts Are Anxious

"Don't be anxious about anything; rather bring up all of your requests to God in your prayers and petitions, along with giving thanks." Philippians 4:6

There seems to be no shortage of excruciating stresses, interpersonal struggles, and reasons to be anxious. Some are better than others at putting on a brave face, but their demeanor hides what we all know is a fact of life—life is difficult. And many days, we find it a struggle simply to push through ordinary chores and responsibilities. A heart heavy with anxiety is exhausting.

The careful reader of the Bible will notice that anxiety and worry are mentioned often. This is good news because it says that anxious hearts matter to God. Certainly, it is important to the apostle Paul. He writes in this sentence of Scripture that we are not to be anxious about anything. The difficulty, of course, is that saying is one thing. Doing this is quite another matter.

Fortunately, Paul doesn't simply slap us on the back, admonish us not to worry, and leave it at that. What Paul does is offer an antidote for anxious hearts: "Rather bring up all of your requests to God in your prayers and petitions, along with giving thanks." Paul is asking that we make God a partner with everything that weighs so heavily on us. Giving voice to those things that trouble us goes a long way in reducing their grip on our lives. Yet, Paul's advice is more than simply talking about our problems. Paul tells us additionally to give thanks, to remember in the midst of our anxiety that God has been faithful in the past, and to realize that past performance does indicate the promise of continued faithfulness.

Some years ago, a pastor in New York City would conclude his prayers by saying, "Help us to lean back into the strong arms of Jesus Christ. Amen." Paul is saying the same thing here. Paul is not denying the power of anxiety. There was no shortage of anxious moments in his ministry. What Paul is asking that we do is remember the faithfulness of God in our past and then lean into that same faithfulness now when our hearts become heavy. There is no promise that our problems will all go away. What Paul promises is God's peace.

God, I am tired today, and my faith is weak. My anxious fears and thoughts are getting the better of me. My fears seem to be closing in, and the insistent voice of doubt whispers in my ear that these moments of life's pain will not pass. Yet, I love you, Lord, and I am humbly waiting for you. Dear lover of my soul, I exhale my frailty and my disquiet into your caring abundance of peace. Thank you, God, in the name of Christ. Amen.

11

Is Belief in a Personal God Possible?

"Pray like this: Our Father who is in heaven." Matthew 6:9

For many, the most challenging part of faith is belief in a personal God. Membership in a local church usually requires a profession of faith. Often, this is little more than mental consent that there is a God. That same consent to God's existence usually assumes that the individual intends to place themselves under God's authority. Yet, what is often present in that "profession" is a sincere desire to know God personally, to experience a relationship with God in such a manner that in those hours of deepest need, we may personally address God and feel that we are heard and cared for. Harry Emerson Fosdick is helpful here: "No one achieves a vital, personal, Christian experience without a profound sense of need."[1] But the question presses, is belief in a personal God possible?

One difficulty in experiencing a personal God today is the tendency of impersonal thinking and living. Anything sensory is found to be inferior to reason and intelligence. During my ministry in Texas a number of years ago, one individual criticized my preaching as too personal and too emotional. He was a medical

1 Fosdick, *Riverside Sermons*, 168.

doctor and sought sermons that would stretch his thinking, not move his heart. He was suspicious of preaching that stirred emotions. To think of God in personal terms, he argued, was unsophisticated. I suspect that the Sunday morning pews are filled with people who are in agreement.

But look at what Jesus does here for his disciples: Jesus takes the qualities of human parenting as a clue to understanding God; asks that we address God as Father. God is not an impersonal force that moves through the universe. God is a living being that knows us, loves us, and has a divine desire for our lives. Jesus draws from what is the best in our hearts to show us its higher ideal in God. Certainly, it is true that God has given us minds and expects that we should be growing in knowledge. But we cannot pursue God and fully know God without the heart. One of the basic convictions of our Christian faith is that a loving purpose directs the universe.

Moments confront each of us that demand more than a mere belief in the existence of God. They are moments of such great personal need that more study—more knowledge about God—fails to satisfy. A calm strength in the midst of life's storms is possible only as God is known personally. The Christian lives not by a higher knowledge of God. The Christian lives by faith, prayer, love, and communion with God. When the soul cries out for a personal God, Jesus shows us the way. It is so simple we doubt its power. Get down on your knees, patiently silence all the voices in your mind, and then say, "Our Father, who is in Heaven."

Merciful, loving God, I need you. I am not sure what these words mean at the moment. Yet, I pray them now because somehow I sense your need of me as well. You need my love, my adoration and praise, my belief in your loving purpose for my life, and even my doubts. You desire to talk with me when I pray; you want to be known by me. Dear God, this is personal. Amen.

12

When God Seems Distant

"I'm convinced that nothing can separate us from God's love in Christ Jesus our Lord." Romans 8:38a

Tommy Lasorda, former manager of the Los Angeles Dodgers, tells about an experience he had in church. One Sunday, he was in Cincinnati for a ball game against the Reds. That morning he went to early morning Mass and happened to see the Red's manager there. They were old friends and sat beside each other during Mass. Afterward, the Red's manager said, "Tommy, I'll see you at the ballpark. I'm going to hang around a little." Lasorda said that when he reached the door, he glanced back over his shoulder. He noticed that his friend was praying at the altar and lighting a candle. He said, "I thought about that for a few moments. Then, since we needed a win very badly, I doubled back and blew out his candle."[1] Though misguided, what a powerful demonstration of faith in God's presence and activity!

Countless people today long for that deep confidence in God's presence and activity in their lives. God seems distant to

---

1 Bouknight, *Authoritative Word*, 30.

them. They plod through each day, fearful, anxious, and burdened with uncertainty. Some may remember once having a close relationship with God, but that was a long time ago. Prayers seem to never rise higher than the ceiling—and that is when we even feel like praying! The good news is that this is not an uncommon experience in the Christian faith. Just as people can grow apart in relationships with one another, so we can drift away from God. As Thomas Tewell once said to me, the difference is that in human relationships, both parties contribute to the distance. But, in a relationship with God, the reality is that we drift away from God. God never drifts away from us.

In those moments when God seems distant, what are we to do? Perhaps an experience I had this past week will help. My daughter, Rachael, is in Norway—a studio photographer for the Holland America Cruise Lines. It's not uncommon for Rachael to work twelve- and fourteen-hour days. Wi-Fi is limited, and with her long hours, it is difficult to "connect" with her by telephone or by other means in real time. Just this week, Rachael reached out to me via Facebook Messenger. She said that for a limited time, she was available to receive a phone call from me and that she really would like me to call. Immediately, I moved something that was already on my calendar to another time and placed the call. Do you see what happened? Suddenly, my greatest desire was to speak with my daughter. To do so, I had to make the time.

We reconnect with God in the same way. We move beyond our desire to be close to God and carve out time from our busy lives to simply be still in God's presence. We open the Bible and read expectantly, asking God to speak powerfully through the words that we read on the page. We learn from our reading more about God, about God's good desires for us, and we learn what God requires of us. We spend time together with God. And we listen; we listen deeply in the silence following our reading to the hunches, the prompts, and the direction we sense from God. As we respond positively, the distance we once felt from God begins to close.

Heavenly Father, you are so very close to me, closer than the breath I breathe. Help me to believe and cherish that each inhale and exhale is your powerful life in me. Merciful God, you are in each step I take, each stop, each joy, each teardrop, each question, each answer, each valley, each sunrise, each sunset, and in the moment of my death. Amen.

13

Our Failure With Prayer

"Early in the morning, well before sunrise, Jesus rose and went to a deserted place where he could be alone in prayer." Mark 1:35

A little boy once explained to his minister that he didn't say his prayers every night because "some nights I don't want anything." Many of us are like that little boy. Our view of prayer is a limited one, reduced to asking God for something. Certainly, Jesus invited us to take our request to God in prayer. But that is not all Jesus taught—or demonstrated in his own life—about the subject of prayer. The consequence of an inadequate understanding of prayer is felt in our own lack of spiritual power. We are troubled by doubt and fear and by a sense of weakness to make any real difference in a world of brokenness and need. We miss much of the strength God would provide us through a more expansive understanding—and practice—of prayer.

In this teaching from Mark's Gospel, Jesus had just finished a hard, demanding day meeting the needs of numerous people. Another awaited him. How could Jesus be ready for it? The answer is right here in this one sentence of Scripture: "Jesus rose and went to a deserted place where he could be alone in prayer." Conspicuously absent is any record of the content of Jesus' prayer. In other prayers that Jesus offered, we are told the substance of the prayer. Perhaps the most familiar prayer is the one Jesus offered the night he was betrayed by Judas, arrested, and placed on trial. It is a prayer that is familiar because we have offered it so often ourselves: for God to take the suffering away (Luke 22:42). But here, in this account of Jesus at prayer, we are not allowed in on the conversation. All we know is that Jesus got up early in the morning to be alone with God.

This little verse teaches more about prayer than most realize. Rather than distract us with the actual dialog between Jesus and God, we are left only with the fact that it was important to Jesus to be alone with God. Before another day of ministry, before another day of addressing the great need of the world, Jesus addressed his own need to be alone with God. Regular time alone with God was the source of Jesus' incredible spiritual power. Here, Jesus teaches us that prayer is more than our formal presentation to God of our various needs. Prayer is a demonstration of a life that is lived with God. Our failure with prayer is that we have reduced prayer to asking rather than understanding that prayer is a real and vital relationship with the divine.

Mark has one additional insight into the wisdom of prayer before we leave this story. Moving the narrative quickly along, we are told that Simon and the other disciples tracked Jesus down, told Jesus that other people, with their various needs, had gathered looking for Jesus, and that Jesus surprised the disciples by announcing that he was going in the other direction. What is apparent is that time alone with God in prayer supplied Jesus with more than spiritual power. Prayer infused Jesus with fresh clarity and focus upon God's intention for Jesus. Jesus was now to go to the nearby villages so that he may preach there also. "That's why I've come," Jesus declared (Mark 1:38). It is easy to respond to the "asks" of those around us, people asking us to meet their needs. It is the greater wisdom to discern God's intention for us in prayer and to respond faithfully.

A Month of Prayer

Dear God, may my prayer today not be about things you have already given and I just need to claim. Am I asking you for things that can never be mine? Help me to be wise and thoughtful in my prayer. You desire most that I believe that I am your child, that you love me, that you have the best plan for my life, and that spending time with you is the best gift I can give myself. Living with this assurance opens up my life, dear God, to see you more clearly, and to love the world as you love each person in it. Amen.

14

Prayer and Responsibility

"Hezekiah turned his face to the wall and prayed to the Lord. . . . Then Isaiah said, 'Prepare a bandage made of figs.' They did so and put it on the swelling, at which point Hezekiah started getting better." 2 Kings 20:2, 7

Theodore Roosevelt, our nation's twenty-sixth president, was born a frail, sickly child with debilitating asthma. At seventeen, Roosevelt was as tall as he would grow, five feet eight inches, and was just shy of 125 pounds. His health, a continual concern of his parents, prompted Theodore Senior to decide that the time had come to "present a major challenge to his son."[1] At the age of twelve, Theodore—nicknamed, Teedie—was told by his Father that he had a great mind but not body. Without the help of the body, the mind could not go as far as it should. "You must make your body. It is hard drudgery to make one's body, but I know you will do it."[2] Teedie made the commitment to his Father that he would do so. The promise was adhered to with bulldog tenacity.

1 Morris, *Rise*, 32.
2 Morris, *Rise*, 32.

The young Theodore Roosevelt took personal responsibility for his physical health and development.

Hezekiah, king of Judah, became a very sick man during his leadership. He had a wound that had become so serious that his spiritual counselor, a prophet named Isaiah, informed him that he should put his affairs in order because he was dying. That diagnosis came like a bolt of lightning to Hezekiah. In desperation, Hezekiah "turned his face to the wall and prayed to the Lord." He pled with the Lord to reward his faithfulness as a man of God and to spare his life. Then, the Scriptures tell us that Hezekiah cried and cried. Before Isaiah had left the courtyard of the king's residence, God sent him back to Hezekiah with another and more hopeful message: "I have heard your prayer and have seen your tears. So now I'm going to heal you.... I will add fifteen years to your life" (2 Kgs 20:5–6). Then follows something that is most curious: Isaiah orders a bandage made of figs to be placed on the swelling. Hezekiah prayed, and Isaiah prepared a bandage: prayer and responsibility.

With powerful clarity, this passage of Scripture teaches us that two things were responsible for Hezekiah's rapid recovery: prayer and a bandage, faith and personal responsibility. If the king was to recover his health, both were required. The Bible refuses to indicate which of the two was the more important. We cannot know which was the most effective. The message is that without either of them, Hezekiah would have died in the prime of his life and at a time when his country most needed his leadership. The power of the Assyrian king, and his armies, threatened the peace of Judah. The death of Hezekiah would have made Judah most vulnerable to their enemies. With his health restored, Hezekiah was able to defend his nation from the Assyrian threat. This story provides an important lesson for God's people: while prayer is essential, it must never be made a substitute for personal responsibility.

There are people who make the mistake of choosing between the two, prayer and responsibility. We have seen in the news recently that parents of a particular Christian sect refused medical treatment for their young son because they chose the avenue of prayer alone. A choice between faith and medicine is simply not supported by this Bible lesson. Each is a gift of God, and each has its own power. Faith and medicine are both means of healing. They belong together. Both are agents of a compassionate God. Prayer and personal responsibility cooperate closely in effecting the highest well-being of those who struggle with illness. This story from Second Kings reminds us not to neglect either. The second-century French physician Ambroise Paré reminded us of this truth when he wrote, "I dressed the wound and God healed you."[3]

Merciful Savior, I am not enjoying the best of health today, and my cup is not running over. Help me to be strong enough to pray, even if all I can say is to repeat your name, Jesus, Jesus, Jesus, with each breath, in and out. Remind me that I am being made and remade every day to personally display your love and your abundance through me to the world. In the empowering name of Jesus the Christ, I pray. Amen.

---

3 Holmes, *Medical Essays*, 365.

15

The Great Wisdom of Prayer

"Early in the morning, well before sunrise, Jesus rose and went to a deserted place where he could be alone in prayer." Mark 1:35

It was said of the disciples long ago that people held them in wonder and awe that they had been with Jesus. To be with one of the disciples was to experience one degree of separation from our Lord. That close proximity to Christ resulted in an experience of spiritual vitality and power. God's love, wisdom, and strength were no longer limited to one's imagination as stories of Jesus' life and ministry were shared. In the company of a disciple—or disciples—God's presence seemed to come near. The vision of God's glory grew more expansive in the heart as a result of being in the presence of one of the disciples. Perhaps that same fascination is what drives each of us to be photographed with those we admire. There is an unmistakable attraction and thrill to standing in the presence of those who have acquired a larger-than-life persona.

In this passage from Mark's Gospel, Jesus had just finished a hard, grueling day. A similar day would follow. How could he be ready for it? What would be the spring of fresh physical, emotional, and spiritual strength from which he would drink? Mark gives us the answer and, with it, the key to Jesus' vitality and stamina: "Early in the morning, well before sunrise, Jesus rose and went to a deserted place where he could be alone in prayer." This one verse suggests the great wisdom of prayer: Every morning, draw from the inexhaustible power of God by drawing near to God's presence. That is done in prayer. Once when a man was asked what he was doing each day sitting alone in a church, gazing upon a picture of Jesus, he answered, "I am simply looking at him and he is looking at me." Prayer is time with God.

The weakest, humblest life can be made stronger when placed before God. As we pray, the Bible promises that God will be there. There will be days when God seems absent. The Psalms tell us this. Pray anyway. Know that God is present. Day after day, the eyes of the soul become more sensitive to God, the heart more aware of God's still, small voice speaking. Eventually, prayer becomes that daily practice by which the individual soul becomes intertwined with the presence and strength of God. The fact of intimate communion with God is the great reality of true, regular prayer. In prayer, we come to see ourselves surrounded by God's love and concern for us as we begin each new day.

How strange, how foolish it must seem to God that we should be content with so little prayer. This particular occasion, mentioned in this one verse of Scripture from Mark's Gospel, was no unusual occurrence for Jesus. Jesus prayed often; Jesus prayed for himself and for others. Jesus took time for prayer before each day and before every difficult challenge that drew near to him. Jesus teaches prayer to us by example, for he knew from his own experience that prayer was a vital part of navigating the inevitable difficulties that each one of us must face. Today, many Christians are troubled by weakness, doubt, and fear, largely because they miss the help that prayer might provide. The greater wisdom of prayer is simply discovering—and experiencing—that we never have to face a day alone.

Loving and wise God, help me to digest this gift of prayer as a spiritual banquet for my soul. My soul will grow from leanness to nourishment; from famine to feast; from dehydration to moistness;

from weakness to strength; from my way to your way; from my beauty into your divine radiance; from not my will, Lord, but yours; from my scarcity to your abundance; from aloneness to enjoying your abiding presence. Dear God, transform my willing mind and spirit today to grasp this powerful gift of prayer. In your beautiful name, Jesus, I make this prayer. Amen.

16

How Can I Find God?

"It's impossible to please God without faith because the one who draws near to God must believe that he exists and that he rewards people who try to find him." Hebrews 11:6

The beginning of the matter is faith. Faith does not mean the absence of doubt. As Jesus spoke to his disciples for the last time, the Bible tells us that some of them doubted. Their doubt did not bother Jesus. What Jesus did was to command them how they were to live after he left them. Here, faith is the determination to live as though it is true. When two people make marriage vows to remain together until death do them part, they are aware of the staggering divorce rates. They are aware of the possibility that their marriage may fail. Yet, they begin their life together on faith, the determination that they will remain together until death. Hebrews instructs that we begin the search for God "as though God does exist."

Faith is not putting aside all doubt. It is determining to believe that God is there, just as we are present in the world. Faith is not putting aside all arguments against the existence of God but, rather, choosing to accept as true that God loves and understands and is interested in the smallest details of our life. A serious quest for God will put away all excuses for not beginning to seek God, excuses such as not having sufficient time to be alone with God each day, and sincerely striving to be in a personal relationship with someone as real and present as a spouse or dear friend. Faith is an acknowledgment that God is someone who is worth our worship, our love, our striving to learn from, and a decision to follow.

Let the one looking for God then turn each day into a quiet place, a place free of the possibility of interruption and distraction. In silence, think of God as present. Perhaps make a mental picture of God standing directly in front of you or seated right beside you. If it helps, picture God as your favorite picture of Jesus, wearing the traditional dress of the Hebrew people of Jesus' day. Some find sitting in a church before a stained-glass window of Jesus helpful, as do I. Imaginatively, look into tender eyes and see arms outstretched to embrace you. At that moment, confess how you have wronged others and God. Pour out your hurts, disappointments, and longings. Share with God your unmet needs.

Then, after the silence, accept the forgiveness of God, the forgiveness you have heard proclaimed from the pulpit, read in the Bible, or shared with you by those who believe in Jesus. Accept the forgiveness even if you find it difficult to believe that anyone can forgive you, even God. By faith, trust the promise that you are forgiven. Trust that God has taken all that you are ashamed of and removed it from you. As God has placed all of it behind you, now make a mental picture that your back is turned to it, and you face forward with no guilt. In that new freedom—and in gratitude—resolve to learn from Jesus and to live as Jesus teaches us to live. Hebrews promises that God will reward you—promises that you will find God.

Dear God, help me not to make doubt the giant monster it can seem to be at times; it is human to doubt. I know that sometimes I want the certainty of neat, clear, and clean answers. And, dear God, I have experienced that too much certainty can sadly divide people, even close friends and family members. Help me to open my eyes to the wholeness you offer and to your unconditional and uncompromising love, my Savior. Teach my often wayward mind to be thankful for the gift of ambiguity, which can lead to strengthening my faith in you. I pray in the strong name of Christ. Amen.

17

The Sound of God

"After the earthquake, there was a fire. But the Lord wasn't in the fire. After the fire, there was a sound. Thin. Quiet." 1 Kings 19:12

My first trip to Washington, DC, was in 1988, attending the College of Preachers located in the National Cathedral. While driving into the city, my eyes fell upon the Pentagon—something I had previously seen only in pictures. Looming large out the right side of my windshield, the impressive structure accomplished the intention of the architect—to communicate the presence of the most powerful military force in the world. Though I am proud to be a US citizen, I am a Christian first. And this military center of our nation represented values contrary to the purposes of Christ. A chill gripped me, and I was momentarily shaken. Not because our nation had a military force. Even Israel has such a force to protect its freedoms. I was shaken by the enormity of its power.

I prayed—eyes wide open, watching the highway that stretched out in front of me. My prayer wasn't clear. My head wasn't clear. I simply didn't know how to process the unsettledness tumbling within. My father served proudly in the US Navy, as did my father-in-law. Regularly I thank women and men who are in the military or who have served. I thank them for their sacrifice and their service. My prayers for our troops mark my daily prayers. Yet, I was shaken and uncomfortable with the large footprint of our nation's military might. My prayer was not uncommon. Many times I have inquired of God about how to pray. I am troubled by this and that and simply do not know how to pray. "Lord, what do I do with this fear, this uneasiness within?"

I turned off of the highway and onto a surface street, navigating my way to the National Cathedral. My speed reduced along a beautifully landscaped avenue; I noticed a public park also out the right side of my windshield. This pleasant, bucolic escape from my anxiety was welcomed. This park now occupied the space that was once filled with the enormity of the Pentagon building. The churning, troubled spirit within remained but no longer at the same intensity, no longer causing a death grip on the innocent steering wheel of my car. My prayer continued, thanking God for the change of view from the driver's seat and thanking God that my unsettledness was easing, though only a little.

Traffic dropped my speed to a crawl. More time could safely be given to gazing at the park. Suddenly, God's hand was on my shoulder. Located in the same trajectory as the Pentagon from my driver's seat was a park bench. Seated on the bench was a young woman—approximately my age—in prayer. In her hand was a rosary—a helpful prayer tool used by Roman Catholics. At that moment, I was calm; all unsettledness had now dissipated. Of the two images—the Pentagon and the exercise of prayer—I was quite certain in which of the two real power dwelt. Each day you and I must choose between the clamor of human strength and power and the silent consecration to God in prayer, between the world's display of self-assurance and the thin, quiet presence of God.

Dear God, I rejoice today and confess that I am a child of God because of Jesus Christ. Alleluia! In this awesome, grace-filled power, I live. I join millions of your faithful followers who live on this beautiful planet and claim this blessed assurance by faith. All of us have become one because of Christ's sacrifice. There is no sign on my face that advertises this spiritual reality. This gift of spiritual transformation is embedded deep in my soul. Thank you, God, for the joy-filled sound in my heart and for this unspeakable gift. Amen and Amen!

18

The Fear of Insignificance

"When you pray, say: 'Father, uphold the holiness of your name. Bring in your kingdom.'" Luke 11:2

Whether anything happens in prayer largely depends upon what kind of person we are. Many of us want to live a life of significance—a life that impacts our world in a large or small way. Such a life is rarely achieved without preparation, hard work, and the perseverance to move forward in the midst of challenges and difficulties. The road to significance is often hard. Yet, to recall a well-spoken line of wisdom from the movie *A League of Their Own* some years ago, "It's the hard that makes it great!"[1] The question is one of orientation. Some seek to define for themselves what significance looks like and then move toward that vision. Others seek to know God's will and then move toward that.

Regardless of our beginning place—fashioning our own desired future or seeking God's future for us—we want to take full advantage of the years we are given on this earth. Robert Cohn, a character in Ernest Hemingway's novel *The Sun Also Rises*,

---

1. Marshall, *League of Their Own*.

comments to his friend, "'Listen Jake,' he leaned forward on the bar. 'Don't you ever get the feeling that all your life is going by and you're not taking advantage of it? Do you realize you've lived nearly half the time you have to live already?'"[2] Urgency has grasped Robert Cohn. Urgency grasps us. Looking back, we make a judgment, an evaluation of where we have come. Life is going by, and the question presses: "Are we taking full advantage of it? Are we making a difference?"

If we are the kind of person that lives as we please, as we have fashioned our future, our aspirations, and our will, then the prayers we make will lack power. Prayers are rarely made unless our plans get into a snarl. That is the occasion we pray. We ask God to get us out of it; God is reduced to our celestial office assistant. Then we move forward with our own small plans. We remain unchanged. Ignoring God for a long time until our plans become jammed up is a little different from being a grasping child. The child asks the parent for unreasonable and selfish things. The parent may give what the child asks on occasion when it seems there is no other way to communicate love. But, as the child matures, parents help the child to think reasonably.

Those who seek to find God's mind and will experience greater power in prayer. Principally, such persons pray because they love God and God's will. Prayer is a communion between two who seek increasingly to know the other, to please the other. We pay close attention to a spouse or a dear friend to learn about them and to know what they like and dislike. Then we turn the orientation of our life over to causing the other joy. Loving and caring for the other is not separated from life. It becomes our way of life. In the final analysis, prayer implies a conversion, a new orientation to live not solely for oneself but for the other. It is a decision to turn our will over to the will of God. There, our lives find their significance.

Merciful God, help me to make space in my life for others today. Through this earnest prayer, you may have to mess up my plans and my way of seeing other people. This prayer may challenge me to go beyond simply saying that I want to follow you. I may also have to

---

2 Hemingway, *Sun Also Rises*, 18.

express that I am willing to be led by you. Give me the humility, gracious God, to accept help from others. I pray for a servant's heart to allow you and others to become more significant in my life. Following the example of Jesus, I pray. Amen.

19

The Deepest Form of Prayer

"Come to me, all you who are struggling hard and carrying heavy loads, and I will give you rest. Put on my yoke, and learn from me. I'm gentle and humble. And you will find rest for yourselves." Matthew 11:28–29

In the deepest disquiet of the day, I am reminded of Ernest Hemingway's words in *The Old Man And The Sea*: "'But man is not made for defeat,' he said. 'A man can be destroyed but not defeated.'"[1] We live in an anxious time. Trouble and tumultuous trials capture the larger narrative of the present day. Jesus is correct that there seems to always be present some war or rumor of war—both wars of combat and wars of poverty, illness, disillusionment, and failure. A thousand-antagonist lineup to squash any optimism we once may have had about life. As I have written elsewhere, we may profess faith, but that faith is hesitant, uncertain, and unsatisfactory. If Hemingway is correct, if men and women are not made for defeat, then some resources must be available to combat the

---

1 Hemingway, *Old Man*, 96.

destructive forces that rage all around us—something more sound and sturdy than the temporary escape various addictions provide.

The Russian novelist Fyodor Dostoyevsky captures the psychological and spiritual impact such anxiety, despair, and disillusionment can imprint upon our consciousness in his short story, "The Dream of a Ridiculous Man."[2] The protagonist despairs of life, fails to find any meaning in life, and is convinced nothing in the whole world made any difference. One evening, a little girl desperate for help suddenly grasps him by the elbow. But he did not help her. On the contrary, something made him drive her away. If life is meaningless, if nothing really matters anyway, then this little girl is nothing more than a distraction. Arriving at his small apartment, he is resolved to take his own life. Before the decision is executed, he falls asleep. Through a startling and poignant dream, he is made to realize that as long as he is alive, life is not meaningless and that the world—in some way or other—now depends on him.

This invitation from Matthew's Gospel is set in a larger teaching where we learn that God has chosen to reveal the same truth to the world. Life is not without meaning, and each one of us is called—in one way or another—to make a difference. When life's storms rage and swirl, and we are disheartened and disillusioned, Jesus offers himself: "Come to me, all of you who are struggling hard and carrying heavy loads, and I will give you rest." Jesus becomes for each of us that inner resource that guarantees that we are not defeated. Here, Jesus is immensely practical: "Put on my yoke, and learn from me." In that culture, the yoke was a symbol of obedience to the wisdom of God. Similarly, Jesus' yoke is obedience to all Jesus teaches and Jesus' call to serve others, to recognize that the world is dependent upon us. To come to Jesus is to learn from Jesus and to join Jesus himself in serving the world in a manner that God's kingdom flourishes.

Each one of us is under a divine compulsion. We must go out and try to take a world that is upside down and set it right. That requires that we lay down our arms of rebellion and turn from seeking our own desires and ambitions and begin to be concerned

---

2 Dostoyevsky, *Best Short Stories*, 214-32.

with God's own purposes in the world. It is accomplished by living in obedience to God's will. It is God who can accomplish the inexplicable. God can bring to pass in our turbulent, confused, and frantic day a peace that is transformative—a peace that recognizes beauty where once we only saw brokenness and heard the cry of a little girl and realized that we could not drive her away. Does that mean a life now lived with ease? Not at all! But it does mean that in those moments when we grow weary from life's strains, moments when disillusionment seems as close as the next breath we take, we can find rest in prayerful communion with Jesus. This is the deepest form of prayer that the disciples knew.

Blessed Jesus, servant of all servants, help me to tap into the joy of serving others as I live my life today, using my unique gifts and my unique humanity. May someone see your kingdom more clearly by the way I live. Help me live in such a way to make someone's life's challenge a little more bearable, someone's darkness dimmer with a little more light, and someone's loneliness and hurt experience your unconditional love. This is the prayer I commit my life to today. In your name, I pray, holy Jesus. Amen.

20

Praying as Jesus Prayed

"Jesus was praying in a certain place. When he finished, one of his disciples said, 'Lord, teach us to pray, just as John taught his disciples.'" Luke 11:1

Some years ago, I returned home from a business meeting in South Carolina. After claiming my baggage at the Tampa International Airport, I proceeded to my car, which was parked in the short-term parking garage. I found a flat tire. Only once in my life had I ever changed a flat tire. That was before I was married. That one time, it took me nearly forty minutes. I remember my father once telling me that I wasn't worth much with my hands. Exhausted from my trip and staring down at a flat tire, I made the decision to call my father-in-law, who lived near the airport. He giggled—he giggled at me often, wondering what kind of man his daughter married—and said he would be there in ten minutes. In about the same amount of time it took him to arrive, my tire was changed, and I was ready to go. I thanked him, we hugged, and each of us said "I love you" to the other. On my drive home, I realized that it had been nearly a month since the last time I spoke with my father-in-law.

Often, this is what our prayer life looks like. Life is moving forward in a pleasant manner, we are happy, and our needs are few. Conversation with God—in prayer—is virtually non-existent. Suddenly we look down at a flat tire, and a phone call is made to God. For many, it completely escapes them that there is anything deficient in their practice of prayer. All that has been understood about prayer is that God is the great giver who shows up when we make the call. Some of you reading this will recall the major home appliance manufacturer, Maytag, and their television commercials of the Maytag repairman sitting by the phone waiting for a call. When our flat tire is not resolved quickly, we question, "Where is God?" Our confidence in the power of prayer wanes. Perhaps even more tragic is that some may begin to question the very existence of God.

Jesus' practice of prayer astonished the disciples. Such was their amazement at Jesus' prayers that they asked him to teach them to pray. As far as we know from the Gospels, this is the only thing the disciples explicitly asked Jesus to teach them. Notice that this fresh interest in prayer does not arise from the study of an apprentice manual for discipleship or from a conversation with Jesus on the topic. It followed immediately after observing Jesus at prayer. There was something about Jesus' prayer life that was different from their own practice of prayer, something that evidenced a greater sense of intimacy with God and something that gave release to more power. As Harry Emerson Fosdick so clearly expressed it, "He (Jesus) went into it in one mood and came out in another; power was released; praying to him was not a form but a force."[1]

Fortunately for the church today, the Gospels have captured many of Jesus' prayers. A close examination of those prayers reveals a surprise for many: absent is any hint of begging. Jesus does not approach his Heavenly Father with pleas for his personal welfare, as though a disinterested God must be cajoled or convinced to offer a blessing. What becomes startlingly clear is an affirmative tone to Jesus' prayers. Jesus turns his back on any doubt of God's

---

1 Fosdick, *Riverside Sermons*, 112.

goodness and stretches out his hand to appropriate the inexhaustible resources available to any one of us. Such prayer retires for a moment from the swirling darkness that may surround us from time to time and affirms that God is present and active in our life. Such prayer, Fosdick affirms, "does not so much ask as take; it does not so much beg for living water as sink shafts into it and draw from it."[2] That is praying as Jesus prayed.

Dear God, save me from the manner of just saying prayers, of using repetitious words, of talking at you only when I am in need. Dear God, help me to learn in the solitude of this moment that prayer invites my heart, my soul, my mind, and my spirit into a deeper and intentional relationship with you in Jesus Christ. I need to develop, merciful God, a strong and consistent lifestyle of prayer, with Jesus as my example. Help me to be more sensitive to your presence as God, Savior, Lord, and friend. God of abounding love, open my eyes to see that you are the only true God, worthy of my worship and gratitude. Help me to grasp that your wise will is being done all over this world and that I serve you among many other persons who are part of your unstoppable and powerful kingdom. Thank you for this privilege of prayer. In the powerful name of Jesus, I pray. Amen.

---

2 Fosdick, *Riverside Sermons*, 116.

21

Hesitant Believers

"At that the boy's father cried out, 'I have faith; help my lack of faith!'" Mark 9:24

The boy's father cried out, "I have faith; help my lack of faith!" His cry is our cry. We live in an anxious time. Natural disasters, terrorist activity, and anger unleashed in the midst of shifting cultural values have brought uncertainty and fear. We may profess faith in God, but that faith is hesitant, uncertain, and unsatisfactory. The forces of evil, destruction, and pain can do that, diminishing a steady and certain faith in the presence and activity of a loving God. Faith may remain, but it isn't the robust faith we desire. Mixed with our faith is a good measure of doubt: "Help my lack of faith!"

This father's son is possessed by a destructive spirit. From an early age, this spirit has thrown the boy into a fire and into bodies of water with one intention: to kill him. The Bible doesn't tell us how many years this has been going on, but the father has now exhausted all hope for his son. Extinguished hope is reflected in the father's request to Jesus: "If you can do anything." (Mark 9:22). It is a frail request. It is what anyone who has nearly given up would ask. In modern parlance, it is a resignation to "what can it hurt to ask Jesus to help?" The father has moved way past desperation.

It is then that the arch of the story shifts. Jesus confidently answers, "All things are possible for the one who has faith" (Mark 9:23). The father finds that he stands before a faith so glorious and strong, a faith that has sufficient resources to meet any need, that his prayer grows larger. Certainly, the father's desire for his son's wholeness remains. But suddenly present is something more. The father seeks to possess the faith he sees in Jesus: "Help my lack of faith!" How many of us are represented by that father's plea?

Each of us has felt the desire to find within our faith the resources to counterbalance the tumult of the world. These are desperate days we are living through. And as one tragedy follows another, we grow weary. Jesus does heal the father's son. And when the disciples ask how, Jesus simply answers, "Throwing this kind of spirit out requires prayer" (Mark 9:29). Apparently, Jesus speaks of something more than perfunctory prayers offered before a meeting, a meal, or bedtime. If we wish to be glorious believers who call upon uncommon powers, we will fulfill the conditions of a more thoughtful, robust life of communion with God. This is a deeper prayer life than many of us have ever known.

Dear God, sometimes I want to join the crowd in believing that by getting more power, more money, and more fame, I will make myself more secure in this life. Gracious God, save me from bowing down to this unholy trinity. God of grace and glory, you sent Jesus into this world in human flesh to show me a more noble way to live. Help me to rise to your more imaginative vision for me. Help me to develop a healthy life of prayer and praise. Help me to climb out of my anxiety into your hope and out of my weakness into your strength. This confused world needs people of your kingdom, including me, to believe, to be strong in faith, and to imagine the possibilities of faith by which you call us to live. I make this prayer in the powerful name of Jesus the Christ. Amen.

22

When We Struggle
(Location: Mount of Olives)

"Jesus left and made his way to the Mount of Olives, as was his custom, and the disciples followed him. . . . He withdrew from them about a stone's throw, knelt down, and prayed. He said, 'Father, if it's your will, take this cup of suffering away from me. However, not my will but your will must be done.' Then a heavenly angel appeared to him and strengthened him." Luke 22:39, 41–43

Recently, this has become one of my favorite passages in the entire Bible. After twenty-seven years of doing ministry, I expected that desiring and living by the will of God would come naturally. It has not. In fact, as I approach fifty-four years of age, the struggle between my will and God's will has become more intense. It is some consolation that Jesus experiences the same struggle here on the Mount of Olives. Such was Jesus' struggle that he asked that the suffering he faced be taken away. I need no further proof than this request that Jesus was, in fact, fully human as we are.

We all face individual moments of struggle. Some struggle with seeking a new way forward after a major life change, such as the death of a loved one or divorce. Others struggle with inadequate financial resources. Still, others struggle with poor health, estranged relationships with loved ones, or any number of new disappointments that come all too regularly. To all of us, in these moments of struggle, the message of these few sentences is loud and clear: do not imagine that because life has suddenly become difficult that you have made a wrong decision, followed a poor pathway in life, or arrived at the wrong place. The idea that faithful Christians always have days without struggle is simply a romantic misunderstanding of what it means to follow Jesus; following Jesus always leads to the Mount of Olives.

It is particularly comforting to know that it isn't unusual to experience the struggle of our will and God's will. The apostle Paul once cried in utter despair, "I don't do what I want to do. Instead, I do the thing that I hate" (Rom 7:15). Paul knows well the common struggle of self-will and God's will. We are routinely betrayed by forces—within and without—that cause us to make decisions contrary to our desire to follow Jesus. In these moments, we may be tempted to abandon hope, throw in the towel, and give up the struggle.

In those moments, Jesus demonstrates an alternative to abandoning the struggle; Jesus invites us to pray on the Mount of Olives. Jesus' own prayer is a powerful witness to the difficulty of the struggle. Such struggle is too great to face alone. Our strength is not sufficient. In prayer, Jesus not only demonstrates his inadequacy to meet the challenge, Jesus' prayer results in receiving uncommon strength from above. And Jesus wants us to know that if we share his struggle, we will also share in the power of God that gave him strength. In those moments when we face difficulty, when we struggle with what we want and what God wants for us, the Mount of Olives reminds us that the battle must be won on our knees.

Gracious God, spending time with you in prayer is my deepest desire. But sometimes, the life I live is strewn with many obstacles and challenges, and it is difficult for me to move forward. Yet, I know that the sacred moments I spend with you help me to strengthen my faith, to grow in my understanding of your wise ways, to be nourished by the fellowship I have in your presence, and to prepare me to face another day. I pray that your Holy Spirit will help me to give you my weakness, my inadequacies, my insufficiencies, and my obstinate need to want to control my life. Your way is always better than my best desires for myself. Help me to live in your amazing power. Amen.

23

Difficulties With Prayer

"In the same way, the Spirit comes to help our weakness. We don't know what we should pray, but the Spirit himself pleads our case with unexpressed groans." Romans 8:26

A parishioner in a former congregation talks about her struggle with prayer this way: "I have absolutely no idea what I am doing!" It is a common refrain I have heard in my thirty-six years of ministry. What I once assumed would be one of the most accessible practices of the Christian faith is, in fact, among the most difficult. Those who are honest, those who are unafraid to express the vulnerabilities of their faith, speak to me of their difficulties with prayer. I always begin by affirming how delighted I am to hear that! If anyone is experiencing difficulties with prayer, what they are telling me is that they are wrestling with it rather than abandoning prayer to the professional clergy. There are three difficulties that are spoken of most, and identifying them helps in understanding this teaching from Romans.

The first difficulty that is mentioned is, perhaps, the one that requires the most courage to confess: the absence of appetite! Simply, there are people who have no driving hunger for going to their knees or closing their eyes to speak to God. We understand them when we contrast this lack of appetite with the strength of other appetites, such as that for good food, the enjoyment of rare and expensive beverages, or the pursuit of some interest, such as golf. A genuine appetite has about it a mighty dynamic that requires little discipline. When they turn to pray, it is often out of a perceived compulsion, a requirement to be a "good" Christian. More time is spent in guilt for the lack of enthusiasm for prayer than the practice. The duty of prayer becomes oppressive.

A second difficulty that is heard is a weakness of faith. Questions fill the mind and heart about the effectiveness of prayer. This is particularly true after prayer has been reduced to "asking" God for something. Though Jesus does encourage us to ask for anything that we might need, Jesus also demonstrates in his own life a richer dynamic of prayer—simply enjoying a relationship with God. That relationship is identical to one we may have with a spouse or a friend. We gather simply to enjoy one another, to share joys and struggles with each other. When prayer is limited to requests, it is easy to dismiss prayer when there isn't a pressing need. God is dispensable. Absent is any notion that we are turning to God with quiet assurance that we are drawing near to one who cares for us deeply.

Finally, the difficulty of knowing what to pray for generates hesitancy. Many days present problems and challenges to which we see no solution. In a critical moment, we are unable to discern which direction to take or course of action to pursue. We are stumped and are unable to fashion a reasonable request before God. It is here that we require wisdom that is from another source—a power beyond our capacity. These three difficulties open us to hearing the gracious promise presented here in Romans: "The Spirit comes to help our weakness." The Holy Spirit clarifies and strengthens our prayers. Additionally, prayers that may be shortsighted or are made without an understanding of God's work are corrected. The Holy Spirit intercedes for us, and feeble efforts to pray become sufficient before God.

Difficulties With Prayer

Blessed God, I live with an attractive and constant flow of stimuli all around me that tell me, "I can; I can make it on my own." As I look over the landscape of my successful life, I am tempted to confess that I got me here. With the lure of all these strong and competing voices, I find it very difficult and a daily challenge at times to depend on you and to place my trust in you. It is not easy to curb my stubborn desire to assert my own will, to seek my own way, and to quell my insatiable desire to control everything around me. Be patient with me, my Lord of tender mercies. I need your available power to help me grow in my knowledge that you deeply care for me with compassionate understanding of all my anxieties, my fears, my doubts, and all my human failings. O God, even though I do not yet fully get it, I will keep praying for the humility to accept the warm comfort of your Holy Spirit to open my eyes to the spiritual value of enjoying you, just you, in these blessed moments of vulnerable prayer. It is in the powerful name of your resurrected Christ, my Savior and Lord, I make this prayer. Amen.

24

When God Says No

"Then he went a short distance farther and fell to the ground. He prayed that, if possible, he might be spared the time of suffering. He said, 'Abba, Father, for you all things are possible. Take this cup of suffering away from me. However—not what I want but what you want.'" Mark 14:35-36

I remember it well. It was two days before Christmas. All the gifts for our children had been purchased, wrapped, and placed under the family Christmas tree. I had the day off and invited my four-year-old daughter, Rachael, to join me in enjoying the holiday decorations at the local mall and lunch in the food court. In one brief moment, she was no longer by my side—something in the mall bookstore caught her eye, and she was gone. As I entered the bookstore, Rachael presented me with a Barbie Doll calendar. She saw it from the mall. "Please, Daddy, will you buy this for me?" Two thoughts swiftly took residence in my mind: First, I could hear my wife making fun of me: "Christmas is two days away, and you bought her a gift?" My defense would be simple and honest: "You were not there looking into those four-year-old, imploring eyes." The second thought was more profound. It shook me. And it caused me considerable pain. For the next fourteen years, until she was an adult, I would have to look into those same eyes and, on many occasions, answer, "No." This one moment became an easy "Yes."

Parenting isn't for the faint of heart. Certainly, it is filled with considerable joy, warmth, and love. But there is also pain. Some of that pain is from looking into the eyes of a child, deeply loved, and answering, "No." Children can't see what parents see. They do not have the deeper understanding of life that their parents possess. The consequences of a poorly chosen "yes" are not understood. Responsible parenting sometimes demands looking into the eyes of your child and answering, "No." Children will not always understand. They will be disappointed. Occasionally, they may express both anger and sadness. The flood of emotions experienced and expressed is unpleasant for both child and parent. But love, on occasion, demands "no."

Jesus teaches us to pray, in the Lord's Prayer, to pray to our spiritual parent, "Our Father who is in heaven" (Matt 6:9). Here, on the night that Jesus would be arrested, Jesus prays. In the shadows of the night, alone in a garden, Jesus addresses his Father "Abba, Father," which literally means "Daddy." Jesus, the Son of God, is frightened, on his knees in a garden, and begins his ask of his Father, "Please, Daddy." What is God to do? As Christians, we know well that an answer of "yes" would prevent Jesus' suffering and death. It would also mean our destruction. For without the cross, each of us would be held accountable for our sins. There would be no forgiveness. Jesus is pleading. What is God to do? God answers his Son, "No."

Someone has taught Christians a lie. Someone taught Christians that fervent, deeply felt, and faithful prayers to God would always be answered with a "yes." That promise is never made in the Bible. What is promised is that God hears every prayer. What is promised is that God draws near to us in prayer. And additionally, what is promised is that there is nothing, absolutely nothing, which will ever separate us from God's love. But God sees what we cannot see. God understands more deeply what we cannot understand. And it is precisely because of that love that God has for us that, sometimes, God's answer is "no."

Dear God, wise creator of this vast and well-ordered universe, my prayer today is brief but no less fervent. Give me peace in my heart and the courage to accept whatever action you decide for my life. You are my God, and I love you, and you love me unconditionally. In the name of Christ, my Lord, I pray. Amen.

25

The Most Basic Pattern of Prayer

"His mother told the servants, 'Do whatever he tells you.'" John 2:5

Jesus' first miracle was in Cana on the occasion of a wedding celebration. David A. Redding, a Presbyterian pastor, declares that this one miracle is a masterpiece to love.[1] Jesus makes an unforgettable impression that he knew how to laugh and have a good time. Though it goes without saying that moments of grief need God's help, says Redding, this miracle demonstrates that gladness needs it, too.[2] What is dominant in this story is not the miracle or the wine, but Christ's presence. Jesus showed up when people were celebrating and having a good time. This says a great deal about Jesus. Jesus came to live with people and to love them—both in the midst of sorrow and loss, as well as in times of gladness and celebration.

From this miracle, we make another discovery about Christ; Christ has both the power and desire to help people, even ordinary people like you and me. It is important that the wedding couple is never identified by name. Their name is irrelevant. They are,

---

1 Redding, *Miracles of Christ*, 3.
2 Redding, *Miracles of Christ*, 5.

perhaps, ordinary people like us, busy celebrating their wedding with family and friends when something embarrassing happens—they simply run out of wine before the celebration has concluded. So, Jesus' own mother comes to him and asks for his help. It is the most basic pattern of prayer: simply asking God for help.

Naturally, Jesus does help. Jesus performs the first miracle of his ministry. But to read this story swiftly, without careful attention to how John, the evangelist, tells the story, is to miss a most powerful dynamic of how Jesus works miracles. Notice that Jesus never touches the six stone water jars mentioned in the story. Jesus turns to servants and asks that they do the work of filling them with water. Notice again that Jesus doesn't draw water from the six jars. Jesus never touches the water at all. Jesus simply asks the servants to draw some water and deliver it to the head waiter, and they do. When the head waiter tastes what has been drawn from the jars, he comments that it is the finest wine of the celebration! The miracle of Jesus, the miracle of turning water into wine, follows when others first do what they can.

When there is a need or a problem in our lives, Jesus is concerned and stands ready to help. But this story teaches us that we are expected to participate in our own miracles. Before Jesus fed the thousands, Andrew, one of Jesus' disciples, first brought a little boy, with his lunch, to Jesus. Before a sick woman was healed, she touched the hem of Jesus' garment. Before a blind man could see, he obeyed the command of Christ to go and wash his face in a pool. To receive a miracle from Christ, each one of us must do what we can. No person's situation is so bad that they can't do something. But it is after we have done what we can that Jesus does what he needs to do. It is then that miracles happen.

Gracious God, give me the humility to ask for your help today. What do I really want from you? Is it so private and so personal that I struggle even to name it to you? Is it so small and minor that I am truly embarrassed to bother you with it? Is it so impossible that I really do not have the mustard seed faith to dream its possibility into reality? Thank you, God, for this wonderful gift of prayer that helps me to be still and learn in your holy presence, to grow my relationship with you, and to move beyond asking to being in constant spiritual relationship with you through Jesus, my Lord. Amen.

26

Hindered Prayers

"Husbands, likewise, submit by living with your wife in ways that honor her, knowing that she is the weaker partner. Honor her all the more, as she is also a coheir of the gracious care of life. Do this so that your prayers won't be hindered." 1 Peter 3:7

During a semester of study in Coventry, England, I was told that a prominent cathedral hosted a guest pastor one particular Sunday. Anticipation of this guest was created by his reputation as a preacher of considerable excellence. The cathedral that morning was packed with worshipers, all eager to hear from a preacher of an unusual caliber. At the beginning of the service, he stepped into the pulpit, looked confidently at the congregation, and spoke the familiar words of the liturgy: "The Lord be with you." The usual response that followed would be "and also with you." However, there seemed to be a glitch with the sound system. No one worshiping could hear the pastor. He grabbed the microphone and adjusted it upward—closer to his voice—and repeated the liturgy. Again, the sound system failed to capture his words. With that second failure, the pastor looked back to the sound technicians, slammed his hand down on the pulpit, and shouted,

"There is a problem with the sound system!" The glitch was now corrected, and everyone heard the pastor. They responded, "And also with you!"

In this passage of Scripture, Peter turns his attention to the relationship between wife and husband. It is unfortunate that some interpreters of the Bible reflect more on the misogyny of ancient times than the primary thrust of these words. The primary argument here is that one's conduct must be informed by a new life in Christ for a vital experience of prayer. Peter uses marriage as an interpretive tool. In the ancient time of Peter's writing, only the husband had privileges. Women had few. William Barclay writes, "If you were to catch your wife in the act of infidelity, you could kill her with impunity without a trial; but, if she were to catch you, she would not venture to touch you with her finger and, indeed, she has no right."[1] The operative moral code of that day placed all responsibility on the wife and all the privileges on the husband. Peter objects to this view and provides a new relationship dynamic shaped by the gospel of Jesus. Prayers, therefore, must be made from one no longer captive to the old world order. Unless we approach prayer with a gospel-shaped life, we experience a hindrance in our communion with God.

The privilege of prayer always demands a corresponding obligation. Anyone who prays for recovery from an illness must match that prayer with a responsible diet, exercise, and rest. An actor or actress who prays for an opportunity to perform on a Broadway stage must match that prayer with hard work in acting lessons and rehearsal for auditions. Anyone who aspires to publish begins by writing the first sentence. Ernest Hemingway once commented, "All you have to do is write one true sentence. Write the truest sentence that you know."[2] Efforts must accompany prayer. Prayer without personal effort is merely wishful thinking or a belief in magic. That person remains captive to a sense of privilege without responsibility. It is a mindset that limits their access to God. Christian growth involves, among other things, getting rid

---

[1] Barclay, *Daily Study*, 223.
[2] Hemingway, *Moveable Feast*, 12.

of those attitudes, ways of speaking, and behavior patterns that elevate self above concern for others. Forbid yourself from indulging in thoughts that you deserve better. Those thoughts are self-destructive. Exchange such thoughts with gratitude and begin to affirm that God is active in your life, seeking to bless you.

The gospel of Jesus has changed the moral code of relationships, the relationship of men to slaves and wives. For wives, this submission is one where men are to live with their wives "in ways that honor her." More, the wife is now "a coheir of the gracious care of life." The marriage is now hallowed and enriched, an equality of both the husband and wife established as sons and daughters of God. No longer are women inferior to men. This new relationship dynamic will be lived in a world that holds a very different view of the matter. This mutual relationship of honor creates a channel for God's blessing to flow. Living as God intends, clothing one's behavior in conduct that is in concert with God's desire for us reshapes prayers that are made. Alignment of conduct with God's values results in higher aspirations that experience fulfillment. If there is little room in one's life for attention to Jesus, there is little room for the participation of God in such a life. If we feel that our prayers are hindered—are ineffective—the trouble may be that there is something wrong with us.

Loving God, help me to understand that I will not grow spiritually if I am all about myself. You want me to grow beyond where I am now. The gift of prayer helps me to learn to take others lovingly into my life. Living with this grace gives my life spiritual beauty and elegance. Open my eyes, dear God, to see you clearly today in others. In the name of Jesus, who lived his life as a willing servant for you, and for me, I pray. Amen.

27

A High-Resolution Faith

"The truly happy person doesn't follow wicked advice, doesn't stand on the road of sinners, and doesn't sit with the disrespectful. Instead of doing those things, these persons love the Lord's Instruction, and they recite God's Instruction day and night! They are like a tree replanted by streams of water, which bears fruit at just the right time and whose leaves don't fade. Whatever they do succeeds." Psalm 1:1–3

Many, many people are frustrated in their prayer lives. They are told over and over again that whatever they need, whatever they want, simply bring those requests to God in prayer, and God will not disappoint. Anticipate miracles, we are told by the faithful. All things are possible if only we believe. We pray. And there is silence. Prayer is attempted again, with a greater mental effort to "believe more" or "have more faith" as though either was possible with greater effort. The silence remains. We are told to blame ourselves. Discouragement settles into our souls, and we drop out on faith—or at the minimum, on the exercise of prayer. Prayer has failed us; we know that somehow we are not getting through to God, so we give up. Worse, without a positive experience of prayer, the energy for a life of faith runs down.

Lowell Russell Ditzen suggests that the problem may, in fact, be with us. Ditzen writes, "We become what we think! Our spiritual health is the result of our spiritual diet."[1] Naturally, that begs the question, "What are we feeding on?" Psalm 1 advances this notion with three quick declarations: "The truly happy person doesn't follow wicked advice, doesn't stand on the road of sinners, and doesn't sit with the disrespectful." This spiritual guidance is immediately followed by two imperatives: the happy person loves the Lord's Instruction, and they recite God's Instruction day and night. Apparently, our spiritual diet—our day-to-day behavior and thoughts—becomes the filter through which we see the world. How is the resolution by which we view the world? Have we drawn near to God or moved far away?

Ellen F. Davis moves this thought forward: "The psalm makes only one point, and makes it really clear: you're not going to get anywhere in the life of prayer unless you're reading Scripture, God's Torah, all the time."[2] A genuine, vital, and effective experience of prayer emerges out of the midst of reading the Bible regularly—even daily—and focusing our thoughts on the question, "What does God require of me?" As we become better readers of the Bible, our prayers are deepened and transformed. We remove ourselves from the company of those who ignore God's purposes and, thus, disrupt God's order for the world. Steeped in Scripture and disciplined in prayer, we are able to see what God is doing in the ordinary moments of life.

Life consists of choices—we choose either a constant attentiveness to God's instruction or a self-centered life that largely ignores God until we believe God might be useful to us. One is a high-resolution faith, the consciousness of God here and now, and the other is a low-resolution faith that sees little beyond the self. Strength rises up in the person who both learns of God and approaches prayer as fellowship with God. Courage is rekindled,

---

1. Ditzen, *Secrets of Self-Mastery*, 22.
2. Davis, *Wondrous Depth*, 147.

insight is broadened, and the power to endure and move forward is heightened. Such prayer pries the "me" out of our consciousness and provokes us to see life all around us in fresh new ways. Such a high-resolution faith leads to a lifestyle that experiences great power in prayer. A people who mastered prayer wrote the Psalms, and it is well that they instruct us.

Dear God, the Bible contains nutrients to help me live a spiritually healthy life and to equip me to grow and survive spiritually in this world. Help me to be a lover of your word, to read it with expectation, and to practice its teachings. I must confess, Lord, that I do not understand everything written in its pages, and I never will. The Bible is very clear that I can walk in the assurance of your love, and I believe that you are with me and for me. Give me the strength and the courage to do the hard work of faith. I invest my heart and my life in your unconditional love for me today. I make this prayer in the name of Jesus Christ, my Savior and Lord. Amen.

28

A Life Trained by Christ

"Train yourself for a holy life!" 1 Timothy 4:7b

A physician once taught me an important lesson about spiritual growth—there is simply no substitute for regularly paying attention to God. He shared this story with me. In the midst of a successful practice as a doctor, he had little time for his wife and for his children. Seventy and eighty-hour workweeks were customary. He loved his patients. He loved his work. Time at home was for rest and renewal for the next day. Dinners with his family were rare. Hard work seemed to pay dividends. His salary rose steadily each year. Admiration for him and his exceptional work held a privileged position in the community. Everything seemed right until it did not. Both his wife and his children had found a way to get on in life without him. "The day I realized that was the most painful day of my life," the doctor said.

The doctor held a stethoscope in his hand. "Perhaps, this is the most important tool for a physician's work," he shared. Doctors study and train to know how to listen to a patient with this tool. What is supremely important is to know what "regular" sounds like when we hold the stethoscope to a patient's chest or back. If the doctor does not know what "regular" sounds like, then the doctor simply does not know what they are listening to with a patient seated in front of them. Doctors must learn well what "regular" sounds like so that when using a stethoscope, they can recognize immediately what sounds "irregular." Once an "irregular" comes through the stethoscope, a decision with the patient is required. This one part of practicing medicine is all about listening carefully and listening correctly.

"I was failing at listening carefully to my life, to my family," said the doctor. "Then, I almost lost them. That terrified me. The difficulty was that I did not know what regular was or what regular sounded like as part of a family." Here is a man who is an excellent doctor but is a poor husband and father. Training was required. Good training is about consistent, regular effort over time. Good training demands the proper tools. "I went back to school," said the doctor. The textbook was the Bible. The classroom was a chair in his backyard for one hour at the close of every day. Reading the Bible every evening, the doctor learned what "regular" sounded like. Then he listened carefully to his own life, his daily practices, and his priorities. What the doctor heard was irregular.

It is remarkable what listening to God will do for a life. A "regular" life, a healthy life, is a lived experience of faith in God. Practices change, and as practices change, a reshaping occurs. Each life that listens carefully to God, in regular time reading the Bible and prayer, redevelops from the inside out. Such a life embodies more and more the way of Jesus. Trust in God increases, persistent hope in the coming of God's reign expands, and love overcomes hatred and selfishness. Life moves from unhealthy "instinctual reactions" to learned behaviors—behaviors that enter the heart from habitual practice in the way of Christ. This is a trained life. A life trained by Christ.

Creator of all things, including my time, in the solitude of this quiet moment, I wait; I listen for you. My prayer in the stillness of my heart is to become more sensitive and open to your presence in my life as Friend, Teacher, Savior, and Lord. You are the one and only true God who alone can reconstruct my often-wayward ways by your discerning word. I need a daily supply of your living water, your Holy Spirit, to refresh my thirsty soul. My inside needs you more than my outside. Open my spiritual eyes to experience the freedom you extend to me by being in your presence today. In the satisfying name of Christ, I make this prayer. Amen.

29

Where Battles Are Won

"Jesus was telling them a parable about their need to pray continuously and not to be discouraged." Luke 18:1

Here is a specific teaching of our Lord to be used against the assault of circumstances and battles of life: continuous prayer. Jesus teaches that prayer is the predominant means available to access the power of God and to experience God's grace. The practice of prayer was a constant in Jesus' life and ministry. After exhausting himself, teaching and healing people, Jesus withdrew to a deserted place for prayer. Before calling together the twelve who would be his disciples, Jesus prayed all night. When faced with five thousand hungry people, Jesus took five loaves and two fish and prayed for a miracle. Once everyone had eaten, the disciples filled twelve baskets with the leftovers. And on the night of his arrest, the night that preceded his crucifixion, Jesus prayed. Jesus urges others to do what he was always doing.

What is it that we do when we pray? Simply, we bring our spiritual enemies, our battles that must be fought, into the presence of God. The enemies remain, and the battles must still be fought. But we face the enemy and fight the battle in God's presence. It is God that changes the equation. As a child, one of my favorite television shows was *The Equalizer*. The premise of the show is that someone—someone who is being unfairly victimized—finds that the odds are stacked against them. The battle was uneven. There simply was no possible route to face the battle, the enemy, and win. Then, through an introduction with a person with uncommon ability—the equalizer—the game is changed. The battle moves from hopelessness to certain victory. What is changed is that the battle is brought into the presence of considerable power.

There are people who seek to face an enemy or fight a battle on their own. There is an admirable grit that drives them. The desire for self-sufficiency occupies every cell of their being. One can hear the faint voice of a child, "I do it!" Unfortunately, many are sadly beaten. Bruised and broken, a reassessment of the enemy or battle is considered, strategy is modified, and they engage once again—alone. Present is a reluctance to accept the intention of God that we never face life alone. We are rarely strong enough for life's enemies or the battles that must be fought. Jesus' invitation in this teaching from Luke's Gospel is that we take the battle into God's presence and engage there. Life's critical battles are lost or won by the decision we make. We are conquerors when the battleground is prayer.

Another dynamic is also discovered when we bring our enemies and battles before God; they lose their stature. Frequently, the enemy appears as large as a shadow that is cast from a light on a dark sidewalk. From one place, the shadow is considerably larger than we are. Such a shadow can have a terrifying impact. It is all out of proportion with the image that has been caught by the light. The result is that we feel diminished. Yet, move along the same sidewalk, and the shadow changes. It may increase but keep moving. Eventually, what is seen is that the shadow begins to decrease. This is the experience we have when we bring our battles before God. We bring them to a holy place where they are rightsized; the threat is shrunk. That is because we have brought them to a much larger place. That is where battles are won.

God of love and power, time spent with you in prayer helps me to strengthen my faith and to grow into a closer relationship with you, better prepared to face life's hard battles. May your Holy Spirit empower me today and help me to release my weakness, my inadequacy, and my insufficiency to you. You offered your obedient Son in sacrifice for me so that I do not ever have to face these challenging moments alone. You are my powerful source of unfailing strength to help me to stand tall and to be persistent in my praying. Thank you, blessed Jesus, for helping me to let go and allow your motherlike arms to gently enfold me and lead me with your tender adequacy. Dearly I love you, blessed God. In the powerful name of Jesus the Christ who loved me and gave himself for me. Amen.

30

The Inner Circle

"During that time, Jesus went to the mountain to pray, and he prayed to God all night long. At daybreak, he called together his disciples. He chose twelve of them whom he called apostles."
Luke 6:12–13

John C. Maxwell, internationally recognized leadership expert, speaker, and author, writes, "Nobody does anything great alone."[1] Maxwell identifies this as the law of the inner circle—the understanding that those closest to you determine your level of success. One of the earliest teachings in the pages of Genesis, the first book of the Bible, is that God intends that men and women live in a manner that includes God in their inner circle. Life isn't to be a solo act, but one lived in the presence and guidance of our creator. Following this teaching, the Bible unfolds the narrative of lives that include God or those who chose to move forward without God. What comes into focus is that one choice results in life, the other death. A powerful plea is heard from the lips of God in the book of Deuteronomy: "Choose life!" (Deut 30:19).

---

1. Maxwell, *Irrefutable Laws*, 135.

In this teaching from Luke's Gospel, Jesus goes to a mountain to pray. Jesus prays to God all night long. Jesus is including God in his inner circle. The content of Jesus' prayers is soon disclosed—Jesus is seeking guidance for the extension of his inner circle. At daybreak, Jesus identifies and calls together twelve who will be called apostles. There is a night of prayer, and then there is a great decision. Our great lesson here is that our Lord took time to pray before he decided. Life also presents each of us with choices, choices that are personal and choices that are professional. Choices that may seem of little consequence and choices of considerable weight. Prayer always surrounds the choices of our Lord, and if we are truly wise, we will acknowledge that we are stronger when God is included in all our decisions, small and large.

What did God do for Jesus in prayer? Prayer gave magnitude to the decision that Jesus would make. The choice of Jesus' inner circle, the choice of the twelve that Jesus would teach, mentor, and send into the world to share the good news of God's kingdom, was a momentous decision. Prayer possessed Jesus' mind of the gravity of this decision. Each of us is prone to live small lives with tiny purposes, lop-sided prejudices, and ambitions that rise no higher than a sunflower. As someone once said, the good is the enemy of the great. Without prayer, the gravity of decisions is reduced to little consequence. The natural result is a life that neither strives for something great nor achieves all God intends. Nothing kills the little things like our prayers.

Prayer also reaches beyond our own limited understanding of possibility. Someone once wisely commented that if we can ever grasp God and understand God's mind, we must begin looking for another God. A God that we can comprehend is far too small to save us! Prayer to God, including God in our inner circle, is to draw upon insight, wisdom, and resources greater than what we possess. When we pray, we move into the realm of knowledge and possibility that we could never have imagined. Bigger ideas, bigger motives, and bigger sympathies take possession of us. Prayer opens the windows of the soul to grandeur vistas where rich discoveries are made, and the heart is stirred to wondrous activity not before realized. Here Jesus teaches that the biggest outlooks come to those on their knees.

All-wise God, help me to really get a handle on this most blessed gift of prayer. Life on this earth gives us pause, at times, as we experience around us our human capacity for betraying the best in ourselves and squandering the high ideals you cherish for us. Prayer opens our hearts and souls and minds to not only draw closer to you, but also to grow in awareness that when we choose you we bring into our lives the capacity to dream God's dream in ways that we could never have imagined by ourselves. And what is your best dream for us? You want us to know and love your Son, who came to earth to live for us and to die for us, and who arose from the dead for us. Heavenly Father, you gave us Jesus as your promise that we never have to live life alone anymore. Jesus, help me to believe that you have chosen me to live in the presence and power of your Father and mine. Holy God, help me to live daily and consistently in the power of this amazing grace. Amen.

31

Ending Well

"Demas has fallen in love with the present world and has deserted me and has gone to Thessalonica." 2 Timothy 4:10

Harry Emerson Fosdick provides uncommon insight upon this singular verse of Scripture written by the apostle Paul: "One of the most familiar tragedies in human life [is] a fine beginning and a poor ending."[1] Demas, a colleague with Paul in ministry, lacked the power to see it through. First, Paul writes in his letter to Philemon that Demas and Luke are coworkers in the cause of Christ Jesus. Paul wrote that letter from a Roman prison. Therefore, Demas, along with Luke, was standing by Paul in his imprisonment—a devoted and promising disciple. Second, Paul mentions Demas in his letter to the Colossians in a rather unusual fashion: "Luke, the dearly loved physician, and Demas say hello" (Col 4:14). It doesn't escape the careful reader of this letter that affection is attributed to Luke but not Demas. Luke is "dearly loved." Demas has become merely "Demas." Now, in Paul's second letter to Timothy, we understand what is going on: Demas has abandoned

---

1 Fosdick, *Power to See*, 1.

Paul and the Christian ministry. Demas began well enough. But he didn't follow through.

Fosdick reminds us that when Luke wrote his account of the ministry of Jesus Christ, Luke alone among the four Gospels shares the teaching about considering the cost before beginning anything: "If one of you wanted to build a tower, wouldn't you first sit down and calculate the cost, to determine whether you have enough money to complete it?" (Luke 14:28). The one who laid the foundation of the tower was unable to finish it. Luke now warns that people will notice that the builder didn't finish what was started and will receive the ridicule of others. Fosdick imagines that Luke is here pleading with his friend, Demas, pleading with Demas not to leave unfinished the work of ministry he had started so well. Essentially, Luke is saying to his friend, "Don't let it be said by Paul that you abandoned him in the work of Jesus Christ."

Has this become our story? Perhaps we have not abandoned faith in Jesus Christ. But how strongly do we feel about a daily investment in building a relationship with Jesus? Recently a member of this congregation spoke to me following worship and remarked that my suggestion that members spend five minutes each day with a daily devotional was a "big ask." I do hope he was kidding, and perhaps he was. Yet, I wonder how many people actually believe that—that five minutes a day is a "big ask." It is no secret that all of us find the time for what really matters. The question for each Christian to answer at the beginning of a new year is this: "Does my relationship with Jesus really matter?"

However beautiful the beginning of our Christian journey may have been, none of it really matters much without a good end. This is not to suggest that we must demand outwardly successful—and measurable—goals or achievements. Building a deeply meaningful relationship with Jesus is not a contest. It is about minding the heart and seeking positive spiritual change or transformation that is accomplished by God as we intentionally nurture our faith. That is done as we spend time with God reading the Bible, delving into good devotional material, and praying. At the conclusion of this new year, it is my hope that it will not be uttered by the angels of us, "Demas, my Demas. Demas has abandoned me."

    Blessed God of all joy, I open my eyes and smile at the radiant sun peeping through my windows. I open my ears to the early birds welcoming the radiant dawn with chirping song. I welcome the happy love of my obedient pet, and I glance sweetly at photos of loved ones near and far adorning my walls. I am again alive today, and I thank you for this earthly gift of life. I am very grateful, blessed God, and I give you praise as I begin this day. Your daily blessings cause me to think of how wonderful it will be when I awake in your eternal presence to look into your face. Oh, what a day that will be, King Jesus! Merciful Savior, place a prayer in my heart for someone who may need your help to look ahead. In the name of your eternal Son, I pray. Amen.

A Prayer for Easter

Shall we pray? Christ the Lord is risen today. And we hear our gladsome hearts sing, "Alleluia!" Thank you, Holy God, for the gift and grace of this blessed assurance! We gather in bold confidence to worship and praise you on this glorious Easter morn. We celebrate the victory this historic reality gives us for the living of these days.

We come in the spirit of gratitude for you have been faithful to us, morning by morning, and in your supply of abundance, our cups are filled and running over, and the power of the Resurrection reminds us that your supply of grace is unlimited. When life's most challenging moments stare us in the face, the still and small voice of your Holy Spirit urges us on to remain strong in hope, to continue to grow in spiritual awareness, and to remain committed to serving others.

We come as cotravelers in this world seeking a little more love in our lives. This is what there is still not enough of. On so many occasions, we fall way short of comprehending the height, and depth, and breadth of your unconditional and uncompromising love for each one of us. Help us to recapture anew today the reality that we are all children of the One Great, Sovereign God, no matter who we are. Deep in our hearts, we know that you seek an abiding relationship with us in Jesus, the risen Christ. It is in you alone, merciful God, that our lives can soar like a bird and achieve our deepest meaning.

A Prayer for Easter

We come as tenants on this fragile planet to be made better and wiser stewards so that in our quest for unabated consumption, we do not sacrifice our sacred responsibility to care for our earth. And, above all, we come to be transformed by your living Word today so that we will go out as reenergized Christ believers—unafraid, spiritually aroused, and assured once again that our faith is not in vain.

With joy and thanksgiving, we boldly enter this service of worship to tell you once again that we dearly love you, blessed God, and that we will faithfully live into the words Jesus taught in The Lord's Prayer: *for thine is the kingdom, and the power, and the glory for ever.* It is in the name of this triumphant and risen Christ, we pray. Amen.

(This prayer, with minor editing, was delivered during the 2023 Every Day Is Easter worship service filmed at First Presbyterian Church of Delray Beach. The service, produced through Interfaith Broadcasting Commission, was televised to a national audience by ABC-TV on Easter Sunday, 2023.)

A Prayer at Thanksgiving

Blessed God, who has abundantly given us much, we pray today for one gift more, a grateful heart. And if our only thoughtful and heartfelt prayer today is "thank-you," we thank you. Your generosity and abundance have made our lives gracefully beautiful. We are joyously blessed with the glorious blue of the sky, the unceasing waves that caress our willing shores, the lofty hills and gentle valleys that dot our rolling landscapes, the faithfulness of your love and daily care, and even for this moment of worship to open our hearts and hands wide to receive the gift of this Thanksgiving Day.

Thank you for family members and friends whose moist eyes we can smile with today. We also remember those persons of blessed memory whose invisible clouds bear witness in this cherished circle of love. We thank you for fun times and comforting pets, for the laughter of children and the presence of the elderly, for touch and taste, for pharmacies and grocery stores, for all those in the food chain who serve to make our meals good to the taste, for inspiration and imagination, for the hard lessons embedded in broken dreams and hurt feelings, for the freedoms in our lands and for those who work to keep us safe, for the delightful dreams in our hearts, and for answered and unanswered prayers.

Merciful God, we thank you for our unique place in history, challenging and complicated times indeed. These present days offer us the choice either to envision and seek a better today and tomorrow or to squander our opportunity in silence as we become complicit with the mad march of evil and injustice and with those whose actions tell us that personal power is their only misguided satisfaction. Remind us, dear God, that we can be people of abounding hope and that we are living in humanity's greatest moment because your Son has made an open show of all shortsighted, earthly powers by his triumphant resurrection. We have everything we need in Jesus the Christ. By faith, our victory is already won.

Mighty God, we thank you for your church of called-out believers. Forgive our so often dysfunctional ways. We are not pointing the finger at anyone, but we are reminding ourselves that it is I who stand in the need of your forgiveness, your love, and your grace. Give us a renewed vision for the Christlike love to which you have called us. May we embrace our responsibility, yes, our commission, to be generous in spreading the precious seeds of the gospel of Jesus Christ, which has touched our humbled hearts. We have been transformed into living witnesses of God's amazing power. Remind us that you are the Lord of the harvest; our call is to be faithful, even if all we possess is one tiny seed. May this church and its members remain unbowed and confident in completing the work to which you have called us.

We make these prayers in the spirit of adoration and thankfulness. We take each uncertain step knowing that you will always be with us. Your kingdom will come. Yours is the power and the glory forever. We hear our thankful hearts saying, "Amen."

A Prayer at Christmas

Ever-present God, your Son Immanuel has come. We join the angelic choir in singing glory to the highest God, and we welcome your holy peace on earth to dwell in our homes and in our hearts. The Living Word of God has become enfleshed, the lamp of heaven has entered our dark world, and the Savior has been revealed. The baby Jesus invites all God's faithful people to rejoice in a symphony of heartfelt praise at his birth.

Dear God, on that first Christmastide, you brought together an unusual assemblage of people and unlikely conditions. Among them we find obedient shepherds; a young couple of modest means and hastily married; a manger scene adorned with curious animals; a season of public taxation; a purpose-driven trio of worshipping wise men bearing precious gifts; a rattled and murderous king; a bright star of fairest beauty; and melodious music in the heavenly sphere. Yes, sovereign God, you own this world and everything and everyone in it. Divine mystery is part of your ways. You chose the fullness of time and place to send us our Lord, our Savior, our Redeemer, Jesus the Christ, heaven's choicest gift, the Messiah for the world.

Blessed God, help us to grasp that we are not spectators, mere onlookers, peering into a historic moment in Bethlehem. In your eternal plan and purpose, we are an intricate part of the tapestry of that holy scene of glorious celebration. Immanuel came with an invitation to each one of us to make the God of heaven and earth our eternal choice. Immanuel's birth reminds us that God entered this earthly domain in the smallness of a vulnerable baby to be with us every day.

As we make our prayer on this Christmas day, we pray for the spirit of worship. Worship engages our hearts with you whom we adore. You are our greatest Christmas gift. Your Son's nativity beckons us into an abiding relationship with you so that we can grow in greater awareness of your desire to be intimately interwoven into our lives. We pray for our often reluctant hearts to be opened wide by your love so that we can listen to your call, which entreats us every day to seek peace and goodwill among all people; we are your lights, your balm, your hands and feet called to give our loving friendship to our broken and hurting world. We pray for an imaginative spirit to share with creativity your abundance with people all around us, even when we do not fully understand why we need to reach beyond ourselves to share your unconditional love.

We include in our prayer this church, this congregation of faithful believers, that each one of us will choose to remain focused on the spirit of Christmas all year as we live in our homes and families, as we step in and out of our professional and social communities, and as we regularly pray for our world, which needs to embrace the spiritual reality that Immanuel is indeed with us. We offer this prayer and praise in the powerful name of Jesus the Christ. Amen.

A Birthday Prayer

Blessed God, as I begin this most special day in my life, I inhale and exhale with gratitude for your faithful generosity to me. The Psalmist David reminds us that you know everything about us, that you are always with us, and that we cannot escape your presence. I embrace this life-giving reality for my life today.

Loving God, this question seems to be playing around in my mind as I begin this day: *Is it too late, or is it too early for me?* I embrace this day with gusto and offer you my uniqueness as I pray for the strength, courage, wisdom, and patience to live fully alive in this season of my life. My God, I affirm your existence, and this belief abides in my heart and guides the values by which I choose to live. I also affirm my faith in the redemptive work of your Son, Jesus the Christ, and I thank you for the Holy Spirit and your indwelling presence in my life.

There is much that happens in my life, unfathomable God, that I do not understand nor can control, but I will continue to live by faith in your word, my most reliable and authentic guide here on earth. Remind me again on this special day that my life will experience various seasons—times of pleasantness and unpleasantness, times of questioning and answering, times of sweet joy and lonely pain, times of ecstatic experiences and dark moods. Your Word has promised that you, my faithful God, will work out all things for good because I am your loved child.

Hold before my expectant eyes that your Word is my light and my lamp as I struggle at times to see clearly along the road

A Birthday Prayer

I travel. I live with the promptings of many internal and external voices offering plausible alternatives. Give me the conviction to make the wisest and best choices that will support your highest purpose for my life. And when in my weakness I slip and fall, I will rise again, dust off my human frailty and give thanks that your unconditional love will never abandon me.

Gracious God, help me to remain committed to my sacred responsibility, which is your command to love all people without distinction. I choose to live with a heart of love being ever mindful that love enriches and expands my life. This is not an easy task, I know, and some of my friends, family members, and other persons who cross my path become a challenge at times to love. Yet, my own imperfections remind me that your grace has opened wide your door of forgiveness to me. I need to learn to love and forgive others because of your generosity to me. Help me in those moments to gaze in humility on the cross of your Son, the innocent and sinless one, who bears all the pains of our fallen human selves. I will live to extend your love and grace to all people. I will ask forgiveness when I have wronged anyone, and with the help of God, I will forgive anyone who has done me wrong. I submit myself to your love and mercy.

Holy God, your Son demonstrated for me the value and power of a life of prayer. May Jesus' pattern be mine as I make my way through this new year. My prayer will involve asking you to meet my needs and the needs of people who request my prayer. Help me to grow in the discipline of accepting whatever answer you choose to give in your divine wisdom. Help me to intentionally increase the range of my prayer. Let me strive to include the various ministries of my church and all who worship with me. The world and its concerns need my prayer; the leaders of this country and leaders of all kinds everywhere need to be guided by your wisdom. I will include in my prayer our fragile planet, our beautiful children and youth, and whatever else your Holy Spirit places on my heart.

And, blessed God, you desire a close and intimate personal relationship with me. Help me to spend time with you in moments of refreshing enjoyment when you and I talk as friend with friend and as Divine Parent and cuddled child. Dear God, I thank you with a grateful heart for this new day in my life and for this new year ahead. Thank you for your Son who made possible this grace-filled relationship I can have with you by his life, death, and glorious resurrection. I make this prayer in his name and with the hope of living forever with you in the eternal realm. Amen!

Epilogue

At its very core, the exercise of prayer is about developing a vital relationship with God in spiritual conversation. This thought reverberates as the central theme of the meditations prayerfully written in this book, and the author repeatedly invites us to claim the power embedded in this awesome possibility. If we can put our fingers on this matter, Dr. Hood believes prayer will become more than episodes of trying to bend God's heart to meet our daily and spontaneous needs. God becomes a friend whom we delight in spending quality time with. Prayer becomes moments of refreshing rest in the incomparable and majestic presence of the Divine. No easy task, but attainable.

To understand prayer in this way invites us to experience the loving heart of God in all the vicissitudes of our total lives. "God," as Dr. Hood has commented, "is never absent from our lives." Intentional acts of persistent prayer help us to experience our daily journey on earth in a loving partnership with God. We are inclined to grow in the spiritual awareness that God is incessantly at work in all aspects of our lives, the big and small, the pleasant and unpleasant. Our doubts and fears do not just fly through the window, but we live with the assurance that God desires more than words from us; God desires us.

God wants us to nurture and enjoy the *imago Dei*, the image of God, in us. Jesus demonstrated for us the quintessence of a life of prayer. Every day we have an opportunity to choose to develop this loving relationship with our God and seek to understand the length and depth and height and breadth of the love of God for us in Jesus Christ our Savior. The spiritual blessings we receive from each prayer encounter help us to understand the divine purpose for our lives; our life uncovers its greatest meaning.

And here is an invitation to this mode of prayer expressed poetically by Elizabeth Barrett Browning's well-known line: *"Earth's crammed with heaven, and every common bush afire with God; But only he who sees, takes off his shoes."*[1] Above all else, the poet is reminding us that God is all around us, crammed into the handiwork of God's magnificent creation. God is crammed into you, crammed into me. God is the inescapable creator who bursts out everywhere in visible and invisible abundance and in compelling beauty.

And here is the zinger question: Can we dare to see the goodness and love of God in this amazing beauty and cramming in our daily lives, in the lives of others, in our world? Truth be told, when we open our hearts to see and hear and taste and smell and feel this loving and powerful effervescence, we will fall in worship before our creator. God's closeness and cramming invite us into a relationship of worship. Prayer invites worship. God's love invites worship from a heart that wants to be humbled before God. Worship of God becomes the center of our very being.

This compact book of thirty-one thoughtfully written meditations beckons us to digest its pages again and again. Accepting this invitation will help open our hearts to become more fully aware of God's abiding presence and grace-laden work in our lives.

Rev. Dr. Leo S. Thorne

1. Stewart, "Elizabeth Barrett Browning."

About the Authors

Rev. Dr. W. Douglas Hood Jr. has been the senior pastor of the First Presbyterian Church of Delray Beach, Florida, since 2012. He holds a Master of Divinity from Columbia Theological Seminary and a Doctor of Ministry from Fuller Theological Seminary. Doug was the 2015 moderator of the Presbytery of Tropical Florida and was a commissioner to the Presbyterian Church USA's General Assembly in 2014 and 2016. Author of numerous books, including *Nurture Faith: Five-Minute Meditations to Strengthen Your Walk with Christ*, coauthored with his son, Nathanael, his sermons and articles have appeared in *Lectionary Homiletics*, *Preaching Great Texts*, *Biblical Preaching Journal*, and *Preaching Word & Witness*. Doug is married to Grace, has two children, Nathanael and Rachael, and resides in Boynton Beach, Florida.

Rev. Dr. Leo S. Thorne is a retired associate general secretary for Mission Resource Development for the American Baptist Churches USA. He also served as a senior pastor for over fifteen years. In his prior university career of over thirty years, he was an English professor and a senior administrator. He maintains a lifelong passion for prayers and poetry. He edited a book of prayers *Prayers from Riverside*, which includes pastoral prayers from senior ministers of the Riverside Church in New York City. He created and hosted a national poetry broadcast, *The Poet's Corner*, for over ten years and has studied and lectured on seventeenth-century metaphysical poetry, with a particular interest in the religious poetry of

ABOUT THE AUTHORS

John Donne and George Herbert. He lives in Delray Beach, Florida, with his wife, Rev. Dr. Yvonne Martinez Thorne, an ordained minister and faith-based counseling psychologist. They are affiliate members of First Presbyterian Church of Delray Beach.

Bibliography

Barclay, William. *The Daily Study Bible Series: The Letters of James and Peter*. Philadelphia: Westminster, 1976.

Barth, Karl. *Prayer: 50th Anniversary Edition*. Louisville: Westminister John Knox, 2022.

Bouknight, William R. *The Authoritative Word: Preaching Truth in a Skeptical Age*. Nashville: Abingdon, 2001.

Chan, Simon. *Spiritual Theology: A Systematic Study of the Christian Life*. Downers Grove: IVP Academic, 1998.

Davis, Ellen F. *Wondrous Depth: Preaching the Old Testament*. Louisville: Westminister John Knox, 1958.

Ditzen, Lowell Russell. *Secrets of Self-Mastery: An Inspirational Guide to the Mastery of Life*. New York: Henry Holt, 1958.

Dostoyevsky, Fyodor. *The Best Short Stories of Fyodor Dostoyevsky*. Translated by David Magarshack. London: Folio Society, 2021.

Fosdick, Harry Emerson. *The Power to See It Through: Sermons on Christianity Today*. New York: Harper & Brothers, 1935.

———. *Riverside Sermons*. New York: Harper & Brothers, 1958.

Fretheim, Terence E. "To What Kind of God Do You Pray?" *Word and World: Theology for Christian Ministry* 35.1 (Winter 2015) 13–21.

Hamilton, J. Wallace. *What about Tomorrow?* Old Tappan, NJ: Fleming H. Revell, 1972.

Hemingway, Ernest. *A Moveable Feast: The Restored Edition*. New York: Scribner, 1964.

———. *The Old Man and the Sea*. Norwalk: Easton, 1952.

———. *The Sun Also Rises*. New York: Scribner Classics, 1954.

Holmes, Oliver Wendell. *Medical Essays*. Charleston: BiblioBazaar, 2007.

Long, Thomas G. *Hebrews: Interpretation; A Bible Commentary for Teaching and Preaching*. Louisville: John Knox, 1997.

Marshall, Penny, dir. *A League of Their Own*. Written by Kelly Candaele et al. Columbia Pictures, 1992.

BIBLIOGRAPHY

Maxwell, John C. *The 21 Irrefutable Laws of Leadership: Follow Them and People Will Follow You, 25th Anniversary Edition.* Nashville: HarpersCollins Leadership, 2022.

Melville, Herman. *Moby Dick or, The Whale.* Norwalk: Easton, 1977.

Morris, Edmund. *The Rise of Theodore Roosevelt.* New York: Random House, 1979.

Redding, David A. *The Miracles of Christ.* Westwood, NJ: Fleming H. Revell, 1964.

Sherin, Edwin, dir. *Law & Order.* Season 4, episode 18, "Wager." Aired March 30, 1994, on NBC.

Stewart, Gordon C. "Elizabeth Barrett Browning: Earth Crammed with Heaven." Views from the Edge, Nov 19, 2013. https://gordoncstewart.com/2013/11/19/emily-dickenson-earth-crammed-with-heaven/.

Printed in the USA
CPSIA information can be obtained
at www.ICGtesting.com
CBHW050719311223
3023CB00005B/16